OCP Instructors Guide for Certification
A Study Guide to Advanced Oracle Certified Professional Database Administration Techniques

Christopher Foot

RAMPANT TECHPRESS

It's the Little Things That Bite You 162
Keep Your Skills Sharp 162
RELAX and Plan Your Attack 163
Don't Be Afraid to Ask Others 163
Instance Recovery and the Oracle Synchronization
Process 164
   Uncommitted Data on the Data Files 165
   Committed Data Not On the Data Files 166
   The Synchronization Process 166
   Roll Forward Phase 166
   Roll Backward Phase 167
Exports and Recovery 167
V$RECOVERFILE 168
Watch the NOLOGGING Option 168
Striped File Systems 168
Data Files and Redo Logs 169
Redo Log and Control File Multiplexing 169
OCOPY for Windows 169
Hot Backup Scripts for Windows 169
Hot Backup Scripts for UNIX 171
Oracle9i – Lazy Checkpointer 173
Recovery Manager 175
   Recovery Catalog 177
   Recovery Manager Backup Types 177
      Backup Sets 178
      Image Copies 178
   Parallel Backup and Recovery 179
   Multiplexed Backup Sets 179
   Backup/Recovery Reports 179
   Database Recovery 180
   RMAN Examples 180
db_verify 182
Conclusion 182

Chapter 7 - Tuning and Performance 185

Be careful with the ANALYZE command 185
Finding Problem Queries 186
Optimizer Plan Stability....................................188
Pinning Objects in the Shared Pool......................189
PCTFREE and PCTUSED...................................190
Caching Tables 190
Clustering Data in Tables 191
Merging Tables to Increase Query Performance..........191
Hints 192
Parallel Hints 193
Performance Testing...193
Parallel Query..193
Tuning Oracle on Windows................................194
Tuning Pack...194
Direct Load Inserts...194
Parallel DML Processing....................................196
Materialized Views..198
Database Resource Management 199
STATSPACK..200
V$ TABLES vs. Oracle BSTAT/ESTAT and
STATSPACK..202
Segment-Level Performance Statistics Collection........202
Performance Tuning Intelligent Advisories 204
Optimizer Dynamic Sampling.............................205
Data Segment Compression...............................207
Using Explain Pan to Determine Access Paths...........209
Explain Plan Output 213
SQL*PLUS AUTOTRACE..................................214
High Water Mark and Table Scans 214
Allocating too Much Memory to the Shared Pool and
Data Buffers 215
Conclusion 216

Chapter 8 - Miscellaneous Oracle Information 219

The Foot Rule of Thumb 219
Monitor By Day So You Don't Get Called at Night... 220
Monitoring Space Utilization and Performance Statistics
Historically 223
Latches and Enqueues... 225
Deadlock Detection.. 226
Unindexed Foreign Keys and Locking Problems 227
Using PUPBLD.. 230
Copying databases between servers 231
Oracle9i - Resumable Space Allocation........................ 232
Oracle9i – Flashback Query 234
Full Database Exports.. 238
Large Table Imports.. 238
Compressing Export Output Files in UNIX................ 239
Terminating Oracle Processes (Threads) in Windows
Systems 239
Truncating vs Deleting.. 239
Copy Command in SQL*PLUS... 240
Displaying Time in Milliseconds 240
!, $ and Host Command Differences 240
Learn Command Line BEFORE Using "Sissy GUI
Tools" Like Oracle Enterprise Manager 241
Don't Write Scripts.. 241
Don't' Write Iterative SQL Statements – Generate SQL
with SQL 241
Input Truncated to 9 Characters 242
Conclusion 242

Chapter 9 - Evaluating Third-Party Products 245
Initial Analysis 245
Determine Impact to the Information Technology
Support Infrastructure... 246
Analysis Evaluation... 247

Table of Contents

Obtain Business Unit and IT Management Commitment
....248
Create Evaluation Team 249
Locate Potential Vendors 250
Initial Elimination 251
Vendor Evaluation 252
Communicate Results 254
Conclusion 255

Chapter 10 - Ease of Administration 257
Good Documentation is Essential..................................257
Follow OFA Naming Conventions 261
Proceduralize Administrative Support for the
Application Development Process 262
Proceduralize the Change Request Process..................262
Create and Standardize Monitoring and Administration
Scripts 265
Repeatable Processes...266
Create Service Level Agreements...................................266
DBA Report Cards and the 360-Degree Review Process
....267
Corrective Action Reports 267
Conclusion 268

Chapter 11 - Oracle Database Security...................... 270
Protecting Data Requires More than just Protecting the
Production Database...270
Identifying Granted Privileges 272
Accounts Created During Database Creation..............274
Wrapping PL/SQL Programs...276
Using OPS$ Accounts 276
Using Security Profiles 277
SYS and SYSTEM Passwords 279
GRANT ANY OBJECT Privilege.................................280
Administrative User Auditing 281

    Moving the AUD$ Table 282
    Conclusion 283
Chapter 12 - Certification Test Preparation **285**
    Introduction 285
    Oracle Certified Associate Tests 286
        Exam 1Z0-007 – Introduction to Oracle9i SQL *286*
        Exam 1Z0-031 – Oracle Database Fundamentals I *288*
    Oracle Certified Professional Tests 296
        Exam 1Z0-032 – Oracle Database Fundamentals II *296*
        Exam 1Z0-033 – Oracle Database Performance Tuning. *303*
    Conclusion 309
    Book Conclusion 311
Index **313**
About the Author **316**

Table of Contents

Using the Online Code Depot

Your purchase of this book provides you with complete access to the online code depot that contains the sample tests and answers.

All of the job questions in this book are located at the following URL:

rampant.cc/ocp.htm

All of the sample tests in this book will be available for download in a zip format, ready to load and use on your database.

If you need technical assistance in downloading or accessing the scripts, please contact Rampant TechPress at info@rampant.cc.

Conventions Used in this Book

It is critical for any technical publication to follow rigorous standards and employ consistent punctuation conventions to make the text easy to read.

However, this is not an easy task. Within Oracle there are many types of notation that can confuse a reader. Some Oracle utilities such as STATSPACK and TKPROF are always spelled in CAPITAL letters, while Oracle parameters and procedures have varying naming conventions in the Oracle documentation. It is also important to remember that many Oracle commands are case sensitive, and are always left in their original executable form, and never altered with italics or capitalization.

Hence, all Rampant TechPress books follow these conventions:

- **Parameters** - All Oracle parameters will be *lowercase italics*. Exceptions to this rule are parameter arguments that are commonly capitalized (KEEP pool, TKPROF), these will be left in ALL CAPS.
- **Variables** – All PL/SQL program variables and arguments will also remain in lowercase italics (*dbms_job, dbms_utility*).
- **Tables & dictionary objects** – All data dictionary objects are referenced in lowercase italics (*dba_indexes, v$sql*). This includes all v$ and x$ views (*x$kcbcbh, v$parameter*) and dictionary views (*dba_tables, user_indexes*).

OCP Instructors Guide

SQL – All SQL is formatted for easy use in the code depot, and all SQL is displayed in lowercase. The main SQL terms (select, from, where, group by, order by, having) will always appear on a separate line.

Programs & Products – All products and programs that are known to the author are capitalized according to the vendor specifications (IBM, DBXray, etc). All names known by Rampant TechPress to be trademark names appear in this text as initial caps. References to UNIX are always made in uppercase.

<u>Unix</u>:

<u>Hard links</u> and <u>Softlinks</u>.

A hard link is a file that points to the actual inode of a file. You can think of it like the actual name of the file in that file system. A soft link is like a windows shortcut pointing to the same file. While you can delete a "shortcut" or softlink, without deleting the file, deleting a hard link will remove the inode and thus, the file from the system.

Conventions Used in this Book

Acknowledgements

I would like to thank Christian Sarkar and Dana Farver from DBAZine magazine (www.dbazine.com). I would also like to than Don Burleson. Without you three, this book would have never been possible. Thanks to Janet and Epi Torres from Contemporary Technologies for giving me the chance to become an Oracle instructor. I would also like to thank Craig Mullins who is responsible for the success I currently enjoy. Craig, you were there over a dozen years ago when I gave my first presentation. You were also there to proofread my first article on database technologies. I have come a long way since then and it is your assistance and advice that has got me here. I would also like to thank Paul Fair, who helped me when I needed it the most.

And finally, I'd like to extend my thanks to the production crew at Rampant TechPress. Thanks to John Lavender, Robert Strickland, and Teri Wade for your hard work bringing this project to its conclusion.

Foreword

I have been working with Oracle for over 15 years now. I have bought it, sold it, learned it and taught it. I am currently the author of over two-dozen articles on Oracle technologies and have spoken multiple times at both the International Oracle Users Group (IOUG) and Oracle's Open World.

I'm presently employed as a senior-level certified Oracle Instructor and senior database architect for Contemporary Technologies Inc. Contemporary Technologies Inc. is an Oracle certified training center and is a member of the Oracle Approved Education Center (OAEC) program. Since my name isn't easily recognizable, I have also included a brief biography of my background.

The greatest accomplishment in my career came was when I was awarded the OAEC Quality Achievement Award. These awards are given to the top 4 instructors in the OAEC program. Like most instructors, I take my teaching responsibilities seriously. It is my job to ensure that all students taking my classes are prepared for the challenges that face them. I try to impart 15 years of tips, tricks and techniques so that my students don't make the same mistakes I did. If you believe the adage "we all learn from our mistakes", then you can truly classify me as an Oracle expert. My classes have often been described as an Oracle "boot camp" (actually it is more like "Foot camp") because I run the classes hard. Minimal breaks and long days are common. I don't want to end class thinking I did my students an injustice by not giving my all.

This book is the culmination of my teaching career. Its intent is to provide readers with a wealth of general information on administering Oracle database environments. The book's topics range from Oracle Database administration basics to advanced administration topics. It includes expert advice on performance and tuning, backup and recovery, Oracle internals and administration techniques including shortcuts, tips, tricks and guidelines.

I did not intend to cover every administrative procedure a DBA performs on a regular basis. There are dozens of books on Oracle administration that cover this information in-depth. If you would like to learn database administration from me, sign up for a class at the Pittsburgh Oracle Education Center here at Contemporary Technologies.

It was important to me to include information that I felt was not covered by other books on Oracle database administration. I did not want this work to be classified as a 'mere rehash' of information covered by others. I have included chapters on database design review meetings, evaluating third party products and a comparison of the most common platforms that Oracle runs on. I think you will find dozens of hints and tips that aren't covered by other Oracle books currently on the market.

Getting Started

CHAPTER 1

Why Become an Oracle Database Administrator?

The Oracle database plays a strategic role in most organizations. Over time, Oracle has evolved and advanced from its humble beginnings as a pure data storage system to a point where it can be currently classified as an application-processing environment that is able to store physical data, business rules and executable business logic. The Oracle database's area of influence has expanded to where it is now the heart of the modern IT infrastructure.

Oracle also provides the communication programs for the client, middle-tier applications and database server. The entire application (data, business rules, executable business logic, database and system monitoring) can now being controlled by the Oracle database engine. The Oracle environment of the future will have a thorough understanding of complicated business rules and configure itself automatically to changing data access patterns. Oracle will continue to push the envelope by integrating advanced technologies into its database engine, offering challenging and rewarding careers to database administrators of the future.

Database Administrators (DBAs) are responsible for designing, administering and securing the enterprise's database data stores. As a result, the DBA plays a pivotal role in the organization. The DBA is often seen as the "GOTO" technician because of their traditionally strong problem solving skills. In addition, the DBA is seen as the IT staff's technical generalist because of the working knowledge they have in many different facets of information technology:

- Data administration – The data administration role, although important, is often undefined in many IT organizations. Those responsibilities, by default, are usually awarded to the shop's database administration unit. Data administrators view data from the business perspective and must have an understanding of the business to be truly effective. DAs organize, categorize and model data based on the relationships between the data elements themselves and the business rules that govern them. Data administrators provide the framework for defining and interpreting data and its structure enabling the organization to share timely and accurate data across diverse program areas resulting in sound information-based decisions.

- Operating system – The only folks that spend more time in the operating system than DBAs are the system administrators themselves. Database administrators must have an intimate knowledge of the operating systems and hardware platforms their databases are running on. DBAs automate many functions and are usually accomplished operating system scriptwriters. They have a strong understanding of operating system kernel parameters, disk and file subsystems, operating system performance monitoring tools and various operating system commands.

- Networking – Database administrators are responsible for end-to-end performance management. End users don't care where the bottleneck is, they just want their data returned quickly. DBAs need to have expertise in basic networking concepts, terminologies and technology to converse intelligently with LAN administrators.

- Data Security – Much to the consternation of many business data owners, the DBA is usually the shop's data security specialist. They have complete jurisdiction over the data stored in their database environments. The DBA uses the internal security features of the database to ensure that the data is available only to authorized users.

Oracle Database Administration Responsibilities

The list provided below is by no means the entire set of responsibilities that a DBA could possibly perform on a daily basis but it should give you a general idea of an Oracle DBA's responsibilities. You can use it to describe your own responsibilities when asked, or if you are new to Oracle, this will help you understand what is expected of you. Those new to Oracle should select a topic and use the Oracle documentation to become familiar with the concepts, procedures and skill sets required to perform the task.

1. Design and design reviews
    a. Application architecture design (2-tier, n-tier, highly available configurations)

    b. General and detailed application program design
    c. Data modeling
        i. Entity relationship diagrams
        ii. Logical to physical forward engineering
        iii. Process modeling
        iv. SQL reviews

2. Installation
    a. Platform selection, sizing and configuration
    b. Prepare operating system environment variables for Oracle binary installation
    c. Ensure necessary disk space is available for Oracle binaries
    d. Assist O/S admin personnel with disk configuration (disk number, RAID configurations)
    e. Executing Oracle's installation program
    f. Failed installation recovery

3. Database Creation
    a. File sizing for on-line redo logs
    b. File sizing for default, temporary, rollback, system, and temporary tablespaces
    c. Object sizing for rollback segments
    d. Memory sizing for data buffers, log buffers SQL area and sort areas
    e. File placement for control files, data files, redo-logs, application programs

4. Physical Object Creation and Administration
    a. Tablespace sizing
    b. Tablespace free space parameters

    c. Tablespace resizing
    d. Tablespace data management parameters (local, dictionary, Oracle managed data files and segment sizes, etc.)
5. Schema Object Creation and Administration
    a. Table, index sizing and creation
    b. User-defined datatypes
    c. Data constraints (referential integrity, check and unique constraints)
    d. Table partitioning (range, hash, list, composite)
    e. View creation
    f. Sequence creation
    g. Hashing and sequence cluster creation
    h. Table, index and view alteration
    i. Adding and removing columns
    j. Changing column sizes, datatypes
6. Space Management
    a. Monitoring tablespace free space allocations
    b. Monitoring schema object (table, index) growth
    c. Monitoring and managing rollback and undo segments
    d. Renaming and reallocating tablespace datafiles
    e. Table and index partition management
    f. Reorganizing data objects to reduce block and file fragmentation
    g. Monitoring log switch frequency and maintaining redo log file sizes
7. Error Determination and Correction

Oracle Database Administration Responsibilities   **11**

         a. Working with developers to identify and solve database problems
         b. Utilizing Oracle features to help assist in the identification and correction process
              i. Log Miner
              ii. Flashback Query
         c. Oracle support calls
8. Backup and Recovery
     a. Creating backup and recovery strategy
     b. Managing archiving and archived redo logs
     c. Tuning archiving to increase system performance
     d. Executing application recovery test scenarios
     e. Disaster recovery strategy creation, implementation and testing
9. Tuning
     a. Hardware tuning
          i. Memory utilization and allocation parameters
          ii. CPU utilization
          iii. Disk configuration, I/O load balancing and sizing
     b. Database environment tuning
          i. Memory
          ii. Disk
          iii. Process
     c. Application code/SQL statement tuning
          i. Explains and optimization
          ii. Parallelization

       iii. Monitoring
       iv. Object alteration and creation to increase access-path performance (indexes, merging tables together, adding columns to existing tables)

10. Advanced database architectures
    a. Replication
    b. Transaction queuing
    c. Distributed database
    d. Clustering
    e. Access to disparate systems (gateways, middleware)
    f. Highly available systems (RAC, Oracle Fail Safe, Oracle Data Guard)

11. Transaction management
    a. Commit, rollback
    b. Distributed transactions
    c. Locking

12. Security
    a. Establishing security policies and procedures
    b. Creating users, roles
    c. Granting security
    d. Password management
    e. Account locking
    f. Account aging and expiration
    g. Fine-grained access control

Code Depot: User ID = reader -- Password = bask

---

13. Auditing
    a. Creating auditing guidelines

Oracle Database Administration Responsibilities   **13**

      b. Implementing selected auditing criteria
14. Naming Conventions, Standards and Procedures
    a. Logical, physical objects
    b. Files
    c. Directories
    d. Roles and users
    e. Security standards
    f. Auditing standards
    g. Backup and recovery procedures
15. Oracle Utilities
    a. Export/Import
    b. Loads
    c. Backup and Recovery
16. Developer Education
17. Process Management
    a. Monitoring
18. Communication Software
    a. Configuring communication listeners, dispatchers
    b. Monitoring number of concurrent connections and memory usage
19. Database Migration, Upgrades and Patches
20. Database Operation
    a. Automating database startup and shutdown scripts
    b. Automating database backups
21. Monitoring
    a. Performance
    b. Locking

c. Security
   d. Auditing
   e. Backups
   f. Concurrent usage (licensing)
22. Change Management Procedures

Oracle Classroom Education

When is the best time to take the classes? This may sound trite, but it is best to follow Oracle's recommendations on the sequence of classes. Take the intro classes before taking the more advanced classes. If you have the luxury (meaning you aren't the only DBA in your shop), gain some day-to-day experience before taking the more advanced classes (SQL or database tuning, backup and recovery, etc.). You shouldn't be asking questions like "What is an *init.ora* parameter file, anyway?" in a tuning or backup and recovery class. Instructors don't have the time and your fellow students won't have the patience to bring you up to speed before continuing on to more advanced topics.

If it is an emergency situation, like your shop's DBA gives two week's notice (Oracle DBAs are now considered to be migratory workers by many companies) bring yourself up to speed by:

- Reading as much information as you can on the class you are taking before you take it. Oracle press books, Oracle's Technet web site and non-Oracle consulting companys' web sites contain a wealth of information. Read the course descriptions and course content at Oracle Education's website (http://education.oracle.com). You may not know the mechanics, but you do need to know the lingo and the concepts used.

- When you attend the class, inform your instructor that you don't have a lot of day-to-day experience. We want you to get the most out of class, we'll help you by staying later, coming in earlier and giving you reading recommendations.

- Familiarize yourself with the next day's material by reading it the night before.

If an instructor sees that you are making an extra effort to overcome your lack of day-to-day experience by coming in early, staying late and being prepared, they will be more prone to help you. Instructors like to see people excited about what we are teaching. Seeing someone enthused about learning makes us want to make sure they get the most out of class. Don't let your ego get in the way of you getting the utmost benefit of the class you are taking – ask questions and get involved!

Oracle9i Curriculum Changes

The Oracle9i Instructor Led Training (ILT) Classes have been dramatically changed for Oracle9i. The Oracle9i curriculum consists of the following ILT classes:

- Introduction to Oracle9i: SQL (5 Days) - This class prepares students for Oracle Certification Test #170-007. You'll notice that the title is a little different that the Oracle8i Introductory Class. The Oracle8i class titled "Introduction to Oracle8i SQL and PL/SQL" included several chapters on understanding and writing Oracle's procedural language PL/SQL. PL/SQL is no longer taught in the Oracle9i:SQL introductory class. It has been replaced with information on Oracle's ISQL*Plus product, correlated subqueries, GROUP BY extensions (ROLLUP, CUBE), multitable INSERT statements and how to write SQL statements that generate SQL statements.

- Introduction to Oracle8i SQL and PL/SQL (5 days) - Although titled as an Oracle8i class, the class is intended to prepare students for Oracle9i Certification Test #170-001 (Introduction to Oracle SQL and PL/SQL). The class provides in-depth information on SQL including information on SQL basics, joins, aggregations and subqueries. In addition, the class also provides information on basic PL/SQL programming.

- Oracle9i Database Administration Fundamentals I (5 Days) - The Oracle9i Database Administration Fundamentals I class prepares students for Certification Test #170-001. The new Oracle9i DBA intro class is much like it's Oracle8i counterpart that was titled "Enterprise DBA Part1A: Architecture and Administration." Although much of the material remains the same, there are a few changes that should be noted: the export and import information has been moved to the Fundamentals II class, Oracle's load utility (SQL*Loader) is no longer covered and more time is spent learning and using Oracle's administrative toolkit Oracle Enterprise Manager.

- Oracle9i Database Administration Fundamentals II (5 Days) - This class prepares students for Certification Test #170-032. The class combines a small subset of the material covered in the two-day Oracle8i "Enterprise DBA Part3: Network

Oracle9i Curriculum Changes

Administration" class with all of the information covered in the four-day "Enterprise DBA Part1B: Backup and Recovery" class. The class also contains information on Oracle's Export and Import utilities for good measure.

- Oracle9i Database Performance Tuning (5 Days) - The Oracle9i database tuning class prepares students for Certification Test #170-033 and follows the same general format of the Oracle8i tuning class with four days of classroom instruction followed by a one-day workshop.

Oracle9i Oracle Certifications

Oracle has also changed the certification process for Oracle9i. Database administrators wanting to become Oracle8i Certified Professionals (OCP) were required to pass 5 certification tests, one for each database administration class that Oracle offered: Intro, DBA Part 1A: Architecture and Administration, DBA Part 1B: Backup and Recovery, DBA Part 2: Tuning and Performance and DBA Part 3: Network Administration. Oracle has changed the certification process for Oracle9i by adding two new certifications (Associates and Masters) and requiring additional hands-on classroom training to obtain Oracle Certified Professional certification.

Oracle Certified Database Associate (OCA)

Two exams are required to become an Oracle Certified Database Associate. Those wanting to become Oracle Certified Database Associates must pass either the "Intro To Oracle9I: SQL" or the "Intro to Oracle: SQL and PL/SQL" certification tests and pass the "Oracle9i Database Administration Fundamentals I" exam.

The minimum scoring requirements and test durations for the Oracle Certified Database Associate tests are as follows:

- Introduction to Oracle: SQL and PL/SQL - Oracle Certification Test #170-007 contains 57 questions. The test requires 68% (39 questions) to be correctly answered to pass. The test must be completed within two hours.

- Introduction to Oracle9i: SQL – Oracle Certification Test #1Z0-007 contains 57 questions. The test requires 70% (40 questions) to be answered correctly to pass. The test must be completed within two hours.

  Note: This is the only certification test that can be taken online at the Oracle Education website (http://education.oracle.com). If you do not have good Internet access, Oracle also allows the test to be taken at an Oracle University Training Center or an Authorized Prometric Testing Center. All other certification tests must be taken at a Prometric (see section on Prometric Testing Centers below).

- Oracle Database: Fundamentals I - Oracle Certification Test #170-031 contains 60 questions. The test requires 73% (44 questions) to be correctly answered to pass. Students must complete the test within 1.5 hours.

Oracle Certified Database Professional (OCP)

Administrators wanting to become Oracle Certified Database Professionals must first start their journey by earning their Oracle Certified Database Associate certification. In addition, candidates must also pass two additional tests: "Oracle9i Database Administration Fundamentals II" and "Oracle9i Database Performance Tuning". The final requirement is to attend at least one of the following Oracle University hands-on courses:

- Oracle9i Introduction to SQL
- Oracle9i Database Fundamentals I
- Oracle9i Database Fundamentals II
- Oracle9i Database Performance Tuning
- Oracle9i Database New Features
- Introduction to Oracle: SQL and PL/SQL

The minimum scoring requirements and test durations for the Oracle Certified Database Professional tests are as follows:

- Oracle Database: Fundamentals II - Oracle Certification Test #170-032 contains 63 questions. The test requires a 77% correct answer score (49 questions) to be correctly answered to pass. Students must complete the test within 1.5 hours.

- Oracle Database: Performance Tuning - Oracle Certification Test #170-033 contains 59 questions. The Performance Tuning test requires a 64% correct answer score (38 questions) to be correctly answered to pass. Students must complete the test within 1.5 hours.

Oracle Certified Master Database Administrator (OCM)

Those wanting to reach "Oracle Nirvana" and become Oracle Certified Masters must first earn their Oracle Certified Professional (OCP) certification. Candidates must also attend two of the eight advanced Oracle University hands-on courses listed below:

- Oracle Enterprise Manager 9i
- Oracle9i SQL Tuning Workshop
- Oracle9i Database: Implement Partitioning
- Oracle9i Database: Advanced Replication
- Oracle9i Database: Spatial
- Oracle9i Database: Warehouse Administration
- Oracle9i Database: Security
- Oracle9i: Real Application Clusters

The final step is to attend (and pass) a two-day live application event that requires participants to complete a series of scenarios and resolve technical problems in an Oracle9i database environment. Attendees will be scored on their ability to successfully complete the assigned tasks.

Oracle9i DBA OCP Upgrade Path

Database administrators wanting to continue to stay current as an Oracle Certified Professional are able to upgrade their certifications by completing the Oracle migration exams. Oracle Education provides multiple upgrade certification tests to allow administrators to upgrade their current certification to Oracle 9i OCP.

The number of tests the DBA must take depends upon their current certification. OCP DBAs must complete each upgrade test in order to upgrade their OCP credentials. An Oracle7.3 DBA OCPs would be required to pass exam #1Z0-010, 1Z0-020 and 1Z0-030 to upgrade their OCP credential to Oracle9i Database Administrator.

Each upgrade exam closely follows the material provided in the Oracle database new features classes, which provide information on all of the new "bells and whistles" contained in the release. Administrators studying for the upgrade certification should focus on the material provided in the New Features section of the documentation provided with the Oracle software.

Listed below are the migration exams that are currently available to previously certified Oracle DBAs (the descriptions are from our Oracle instructor's website):

- Upgrade Exam: Oracle7.3 to Oracle8 OCP DBA (#1Z0-010). - This exam covers information provided in the Oracle8 New Features for Administrators class. The exam focuses on partitioned tables and indexes, parallelizing INSERT, UPDATE and DELETE operations, extended ROWIDS, defining object-relational objects, managing large objects (i.e. LOBS, CLOBS), advanced queuing, index organized tables and Oracle8 security enhancements.

- Upgrade Exam: Oracle8 to Oracle8i OCP DBA (#1Z0-020) - The Oracle8i upgrade exam covers information provided by the Oracle8i New Features for Administrators class. This exam focuses on the Oracle Java implementation, optimizer and query performance improvements, materialized views, bitmap index and index-organized enhancements and range, hash and composite partitioning. The exam also covers Oracle installer enhancements, locally managed tablespaces, transportable tablespaces and the Oracle8i database resource manager.

- Upgrade Exam: Oracle8i to Oracle9i OCP DBA (#1Z0-030) - Like its aforementioned counterparts, the Oracle9i upgrade covers information provided by the Oracle9i New Features for Administrators Class. The exam covers information on fine grained auditing, partitioned fine grained access control, secure application roles, global context, flashback query, resumable space allocation, SPFILEs, log miner enhancements and recovery manager new features.

Other Recommend Classes

Oracle Education provides dozens of additional classes on Oracle technologies. These additional classes provide more in-depth information in key areas of database administration. A few recommendations on additional classes follow (the course descriptions are straight from our instructor's website):

- Oracle9I Program with PL/SQL. An excellent class for database administrators wanting to learn more about Oracle's procedural language. This course introduces students to PL/SQL and helps them understand the benefits of this powerful programming language. Students learn to create stored procedures, SQL functions, packages, and database triggers.

- Oracle9i Database: SQL Tuning Workshop R2. This course is designed to give the student a firm foundation in the art of SQL tuning. The participant learns the skills and toolsets used to effectively tune SQL statements. The course contains numerous workshops that allow students to practice their SQL tuning skills. The students learn EXPLAIN, SQL Trace and TKPROF, SQL*Plus AUTOTRACE.

- Oracle Enterprise Manager 9i. This course is taught on Oracle9i Release 2. Students learn how to use Oracle Enterprise Manager to effectively administer a multiple database environment. This class is a must attend for those that want to make sure that they are utilizing Oracle Enterprise Manager to its fullest potential.

- Oracle9i: New Features for Administrators R2. This course introduces students to the new features in contained in Oracle9i. All of the latest features are discussed and tested.

- Managing Oracle on Linux. Students learn how to configure and administer the Oracle9i database on Linux. Database creation, configuration, automated startup/shutdown scripts, file system choices are just a few of the topics covered in this class. Hands-on lab exercise help students reinforce the knowledge obtained from lectures.

Preparing for the Oracle Certified Professional Exams

The best time to take the exam is a week or two after taking the Oracle class that the exam pertains to. Passing the certification test is much easier when the information is fresh. The class workbook should be used as the primary study guide. I have passed every exam I have taken by studying only the information contained in the class workbooks. The classes are not required to obtain Oracle9i OCP certification, but the requirements have changed for Oracle9i OCP certification (see Oracle9i Oracle Certifications above).

The Oracle Education website (http://education.oracle.com) allows administrators to purchase practice exam tests. Free sample questions are also available. Practice tests provide the administrator with a firm understanding of the areas that they are strong in as well as the areas where they need to shore up their knowledge.

The Oracle provided practice tests provide a thorough coverage of the Oracle certification requirements and use the same test question technology as the real exams including simulations, scenarios, hot spots and case studies. Other practice test features include:

- Tutorials and text references that enhance the learning process.
- Random generation of test questions provides a dynamic and challenging testing environment.

- Testing and grading by objective to allow administrators to focus on specific areas.
- Thorough review of all answers (both correct and incorrect).
- More questions provided than any other source.

Taking the Certification Exams

Oracle partners with Prometric Testing Centers to provide testing centers throughout the United States. The Prometric Testing Center website (http://www.2test.com/) provides a test center locator to help you find testing centers in your area.

The following hints and tips will prepare you for the day you take your certification tests:

- You must have two forms of identification, both containing your signature. One must be a government issued photo identification.
- Try to show up early (at least 15 minutes) before your scheduled exam. If you show up more than 15 minutes late, the testing center coordinator has the option of canceling your exam and asking you to reschedule your test.
- You cannot bring any notes or scratch paper to the testing center. Paper will be provided by the testing center and will be destroyed when you leave.
- Testing center personnel will provide you with a brief overview of the testing process. The computer will have a demo that will show you how to answer and review test questions.

- Don't leave any questions unanswered. All test questions left unanswered will be marked as incorrect.

- Your exam score is provided to you immediately and the exam results are forwarded to Oracle Certification Program management. Make sure you keep a copy of your test results for your records.

- If you fail a test, you must wait at least 30 days before retaking it (except for exam #1Z0-007 Introduction to Oracle9i: SQL).

Finding Information Quickly – The Key to Success

If you remember anything from this whitepaper, make it the following statement:

> The hallmark of a being a good DBA is not knowing everything, but knowing where to look when you don't.

But there is so much information available on Oracle that it tends to become overwhelming. How do you find that one facet of information, that one explanation you are looking for when you are confronted with seemingly endless sources of information? Here's a hint, GO TO THE MANUALS FIRST. The Concepts manual is a good start, closely followed by the SQL*PLUS Users Guide, the Administrator's Guide, the Reference manual and the SQL Reference manual. The next two should be Oracle Backup and Recovery Concepts and the Oracle Enterprise Manager User's Reference Manual. If you don't find the information you are looking for in

Oracle's Technical Reference Guides, then look elsewhere. Whether you have been burned or not, you must trust the information they provide. This paper will provide you with alternative sources of information but they are NOT intended to be substitutions for the vendor's reference guides.

A very experienced co-worker of mine was at a customer site installing an Oracle9i database on LINUX. He was reading the installation manual when the customer demanded to know why he was reading the manual when he was supposed to be "the high-priced expert." He quickly replied, "I'm reading the manual because I am an expert." As your experience grows, you'll find that you'll become just like my co-worker, an avid user of the reference guides and not afraid to admit it.

Reference Manuals

It is good practice to keep a set of reference manuals for each major release of the database you are administering. Oracle does have a tendency to change default values for object specifications. In addition, each new release contains new parameters that affect the database's configuration. When you receive the latest and greatest version of Oracle's database (one of the benefits of purchasing support), turn straight to the "OracleX New Features" section to find out what impact the new release will have on your daily administrative activities. You'll also find many new features that haven't been covered by Oracle's new release whitepapers and marketing propaganda.

Oracle Internal Resources

The Oracle websites contain a wealth of information on the Oracle product sets. The trick is knowing where to look. Some may think that Oracle webmasters rewrite the websites from time to time just to make it challenging for us to find the information we are looking for.

The following Oracle websites are favorites of mine and are ranked according to my personal preference:

- metalink.oracle.com - Oracle's premier web support service is available to all customers who have current support service contracts. Oracle MetaLink allows customers to log and track service requests. Metalink also allows users to search Oracle's support and bug databases. When you experience an Oracle problem, look up the return code (if one is provided) in the Oracle reference manuals. If you are unable to solve the problem, search the Metalink bug database using the return code or error message as the search criteria. The website also contains a patch and patchset download area, product availability and life cycle information and technical libraries containing whitepapers and informational documents.

- docs.oracle.com – Oracle's technical reference manual website. This website stores technical reference manuals for Oracle7, Oracle8, Oracle8i, Oracle9i, Oracle RDB, Oracle Gateways and Applications 10.7, 11 and 11i. A quick and easy way to get access to the information you need.

- partner.oracle.com – If you are an Oracle partner, (and there are a lot of us), then this is the website for you. Oracle's partner website contains information on partner initiatives and provides customized portlets categorized into partner activity and job role.

- technet.oracle.com - Technet's software download area allows visitors to download virtually any product Oracle markets. Visitors are also able to view Oracle documentation, download product whitepapers, search for jobs that use Oracle technologies and obtain information on Oracle education.

- education.oracle.com – Oracle University's web site contains information on Oracle education including course descriptions, class schedules, self-study courses and certification requirements.

- www.oracle.com - Oracle's home page on the web.

External Resources

Non-Oracle websites are also excellent sources of information. The Internet has an abundance of web sites containing hundreds of scripts, tips, tricks and techniques. Some of my favorites are:

- www.dbazine.com - How can you not love this website? The contributing authors list reads like a "who's who" of the database industry. Topics range from entry-level discussions to information that even the most experienced database user would find enlightening. Experts like Mullins, Inmon, Ensor, Celko and Burleson provide readers with articles that are topical and interesting. Great articles and a pleasing, easy-to-navigate website makes DBAZine the place to go for database information.

- www.orafaq.com - Orafaq discussion forums are excellent sources of information. Post a question to hundreds of experienced Oracle DBAs and you'll find out just how helpful Orafaq can be. Orafaq provides an intelligent search engine that visitors can use to search the discussion forums for topics of interest. The website also provides hints, tips, scripts, whitepapers and an on-line chatroom.

- www.oracle.com/oramag - Oracle Corporation's own technical magazine. Oracle Magazine provides readers with product announcements, customer testimonials, technical information and upcoming events. Oracle magazine is available in hardcopy and on the web.

- www.lazydba.com - Why write scripts when you can download them from the web? There are numerous web sites to choose from but this site is one of my favorites. The scripts are written by numerous contributors and, on the whole, well written. Find the script that solves your problem, download it, test and implement!

- www.orsweb.com - Another excellent site that contains dozens of useful scripts.

Book Recommendations

Third-party books are another excellent source of information. The big advantage third-party books have over the technical reference manuals is that they are able to quickly deliver the information that most of us feel is important. Technical reference manuals must provide all of the information on the entire Oracle environment while third-party books are able to focus on just what the author felt was important.

Instead of listing books, I'll list my favorite authors. You'll have the best chance of buying a great book if you select one from the following authors: any of the experts from TUSC, Don Burleson (even though TUSC and Burleson are competitors), Michael Ault, Michael Abbey, George Koch, and Kevin Loney.

Don Burleson, a long-time contributor to DBAZine.com, is one of my favorite authors on Oracle Technologies. I currently own more books from him than any other technical author. My current favorites are the *Oracle9i High-Performance Tuning with STATSPACK* and the *Oracle9i: UNIX Administration Handbook*.

Don has written 14 books (last count anyway) and has published more than 100 articles in national magazines. Don's experience in both Oracle and writing allows him to transform highly technical information into easily understood (and interesting) text. When I find the need to refresh my knowledge on a particular topic, I find myself going first to one of Don's books.

Who do I think has the greatest ability to transfer technical information to the reader? Craig Mullins is a well-known DB2 expert and author of the *DB2 Developer's Guide*. Craig has just written one of my favorite administration books of all time, *Database Administration – The Compete Guide to Practices and Procedures*. This book covers all databases and WILL make you a better DBA. Don't worry that Craig is an expert in a competing product, he is not just a DB2 expert, Craig is one of the few people I know that are qualified to be a true database expert.

Conclusion

In this chapter, we learned that becoming an Oracle DBA is much more than being a "table jockey". We now know database administrators plays a pivotal role in the IT organization and are involved in all aspects of the application development process. The DBA of today must have a strong understanding of the business processes as well as the technical intricacies of the Oracle environment to be successful. The DBA is truly the conduit between the business personnel that use the application and the technical units that support them. The administrator is able to discuss complex business topics with application developers and business users and then switch to "techno jargon" to discuss in-depth technical issues with infrastructure support units.

We also learned the importance of education and becoming certified. Oracle certifications, once known as something "nice to have", are becoming job requirements. The key to successful test taking is to understand the requirements of the test and study, study, study. I have seen administrators with years of experience fail entry-level certification tests because of a lack of preparation.

One final thought bears repeating. "The hallmark of a being a good DBA is not knowing everything, but knowing where to look when you don't." Read the Oracle manuals and trust the information they provide. They contain virtually everything you need to know to successfully administer an Oracle database. Only after becoming well versed in the documentation should you begin reading third-party offerings.

In the next chapter, we will learn that an application is only as good as the database architecture that it runs on. Chapter two starts with an in-depth discussion of the three most popular operating systems (Windows, Linux, UNIX) and ends with an operating system comparison table.

Oracle Database Architectures

CHAPTER 2

Oracle Database Architectures

Choosing the correct database architecture (hardware platform, operating system) is critical to the success of any new Oracle database application. Architecture decisions were simple when the mainframe was the only architecture available. But architecture selection is not as clear-cut now that Microsoft Windows platforms, UNIX and LINUX are viable database environments. Oracle is more than happy to offer their flagship database on a wide-variety of hardware and operating system combinations. As a result, IT shops have more hardware and software choices available to them than ever before. The key to success is choosing the right ones.

A correctly chosen architecture will result in an application that performs to expectations, scales easily to meet increased user demands, and is easily administered. Incorrect architecture decisions may result in poor performance, limited functionality, complex administration and tuning, lack of scalability, poor vendor support, poor reliability and availability and a high total cost of ownership.

Architecture decisions should not be made in a vacuum or based on personal preference. It is important for all large IT shops to create a part-time architecture selection team consisting of members drawn from the following areas: LAN/WAN communications, O/S support, operations, architectures and database administration. This team should be responsible for determining the best architecture for a particular application.

Extensive up-front analysis is critical during the architecture selection process, so let's continue our discussion on Oracle database architectures by comparing three of the more popular Oracle database platforms: Oracle on Windows, Oracle on LINUX and Oracle on Unix. We'll conclude with a database architecture comparison chart that compares the Windows, LINUX and Unix architectures.

Oracle on Microsoft Windows Platforms

Microsoft Window's success as a server operating systems began when Microsoft released SQL Server 4.2 for the Windows NT operating system in 1994. Microsoft SQL Server 4.2 was a full-function relational database server with an attractive price tag. The traditional database competitors (Oracle, Informix, Sybase, IBM) realized that in order to compete in the departmental arena, they must begin to market a scaled down (and cheaper) version of their enterprise UNIX databases. Some of the workgroup database server products were simply the vendor's flagship enterprise database repackaged and re-priced to appeal to a different group of customers.

Database vendor competition is fierce in this environment. Microsoft's attempt to dominate this architecture tier with SQLServer is forcing all vendors to adjust pricing and accelerate the release of new products as well as enhancements to existing products. This high level of competition between vendors allows consumers to take advantage of a high level of functionality at a reasonable cost.

The Windows server operating systems are known for their low-cost and ease-of-use. The Windows operating system is more easily administered than UNIX and Linux. Windows servers use the same type of interface as their Windows client operating systems counterparts. Administrators are able to perform a large percentage of their administrative duties through a familiar point-and-click GUI interface. Windows operating system manuals use familiar PC terminology when discussing concepts of general administration. Some flavors of UNIX have GUI administrative tools, but the majority of administrative duties are still performed via command line interface using rather cryptic operating system commands (*grep, awk, ps -ef, cat*).

Database vendors realize that Windows servers oftentimes exist outside of the traditional information processing support framework. As a result, general ease of use is not a competitive advantage but a competitive requirement. Windows database products can be characterized by their easy installation, ease of use, limited tuning options, and good documentation. All vendors offer strong visual administration and monitoring tools that do not require the administration skill and intimate knowledge of the database required by their UNIX and LINUX counterparts.

The fastest Windows database title moves from vendor to vendor due to strong vendor competition and fast paced advancements in hardware and operating systems. Microsoft and Intel hardware vendor's clustering technologies allow technicians to connect multiple hardware platforms together and make them appear to end-users as a single-image environment. Clustering provides Windows environments with both scale-up (scalability within the hardware chassis by adding hardware components) and scale-out (scalability by adding additional hardware chassis) capabilities.

Although not as easily measured as performance, reliability must be considered when evaluating database architectures. In the beginning, the majority of consumers rarely considered Windows NT to be a viable alternative in this arena. Consumers' faith in Windows reliability is growing as the Windows operating system family matures and new functionality is added by Microsoft, hardware vendors, and third-party software solutions providers. Oracle offers highly available solutions for Windows environments with its Oracle Data Guard, Oracle Fail Safe and Oracle RAC for Windows product sets.

Oracle on LINUX Platforms

Running Oracle on LINUX/Intel platforms is rapidly gaining in popularity. The Oracle Corporation is fostering LINUX's credibility as a mission-critical operating system by being the first vendor to market both an enterprise relational database and an enterprise application server for the operating system.

Oracle, Dell and Red Hat have formed a partnership to to enhance the LINUX/Intel environment in the areas of performance, reliability, clustering, and manageability. The three partners are collaborating to develop and market enterprise-ready LINUX solutions based on Dell PowerEdge Servers, Dell/EMC and PowerVault storage systems, Oracle9i Database Release 2 with Real Application Clusters, and Red Hat LINUX Advanced Server.

Oracle also provides direct support for the Red Hat LINUX Advanced Server operating system. Oracle customers who use the Red Hat LINUX Advanced Server operating system will be able to call Oracle support for both LINUX and Oracle issues.

LINUX combines the ease of use and cost-effectiveness of Intel hardware platforms with the performance, reliability and availability of enterprise-class UNIX servers. If the application requires more processing power, CPUs, memory and disk can be purchased without making a major impact on the business unit's operating budget. LINUX is designed to be user-friendly and easy to install. LINUX can be installed on a home PC as well as a network server for a fraction of the cost of competing software packages.

Compared to their Windows and UNIX counterparts, the majority of LINUX vendors have only recently begun to expend resources on providing highly available architectures to consumers desiring fault tolerant systems for mission-critical applications. The reasons for this lack of focus are:

- The LINUX operating system is relatively new and has only become recently popular with corporate consumers. Historically, large corporations have not considered LINUX as a viable corporate operating system. One can only assume that most corporations felt that anything that was free wasn't a viable product. Only when Red Hat and other competing vendors began to formalize and "corporatize" their LINUX offerings did corporate consumers begin to consider LINUX as an alternative to Windows and UNIX.

- Consumer perception (or misconception) that the UNIX operating systems are inherently more reliable than their LINUX counterparts resulting in a lack of consumer demand for highly available LINUX servers.

- Market analysis showing that product cost and not high availability being the primary reason consumers choose LINUX environments.

- The cost of highly available LINUX servers approaching the bottom tier prices of enterprise Unix environments that have many fault tolerant features inherent to their architectures.

- LINUX hardware server platforms not being perceived by some consumers as highly available when compared to competing UNIX hardware offerings from Sun, HP, IBM, etc.

Will LINUX continue to gain in popularity? The answer is absolutely! LINUX growth will continue to be fed by the rapidly improving price/performance ratio of Intel server hardware and the increasing acceptance of LINUX as an enterprise-ready operating system by both corporate consumers and third-party application vendors.

Oracle on Unix Platforms

Unlike LINUX, which has only recently become popular, UNIX platforms have been the perennial favorites of shops desiring to build non-mainframe applications. UNIX platforms were the only alternative to mainframes before Microsoft Windows and LINUX evolved into viable alternatives.

Sun, HP, Data General and Sequent were competing for the corporate consumer's dollar years before the client/server revolution popularized non-mainframe architectures. As a result, there are a large number of third party tools and applications available for UNIX architectures. In addition, competition between hardware and database vendors in this environment is fierce, resulting in rapid advances in technology and features.

UNIX databases lead all other architectures in database software options and add-ons available to consumers. Hardware vendor (HP, SUN, IBM, etc.) competition in this tier is fierce. Because of this competition, hardware vendors are required to release new hardware and O/S features on a regular basis to survive, making this tier the most technically advanced of the three. Performance and reliability are the key advantages of this environment, while cost and complex administration are the drawbacks.

Traditional UNIX vendors (with Sun leading the way) realize that to compete against Windows and LINUX they must make their operating systems easier to use. Most UNIX operating systems now provide GUI administrative tools, but the majority of administrative duties are still performed via command line interface using rather cryptic operating system commands (*grep, awk, ps -ef, cat*).

Although alike in many ways, each UNIX operating system has its own variations of system commands, administrative processes and procedures. This complicates application development, operating system support, and database administration for shops that run different versions of the UNIX operating system. Operating system administrators are unable to make a seamless transition from one environment to another and administrators must be trained in each operating system to effectively administer it.

Performance is a key selling point for vendors in this environment and as a result, enterprise UNIX hardware, operating systems and database software are all designed for high performance. High-end enterprise servers have the capability of supporting hundreds of gigabytes of disk and can certainly support many hundreds of users. Until recently, the majority TPC-C and TPC-D benchmark records were held by hardware platforms running some flavor of the UNIX operating system. Windows and Linux are now beginning to challenge UNIX's position as performance leader, recently capturing several TPC-C and TPC-D benchmarks.

All enterprise UNIX vendors must stress reliability to be competitive in the enterprise marketplace. In addition, many offer additional products that take advantage of UNIX clustering services. UNIX has almost thirty years of continuous development, making it the most mature of all operating systems with a proven track record of reliability.

The chart below provides a quick, high-level comparison of the three major operating systems in use today.

Database Architecture Comparison Worksheet

CRITERIA/ ARCHITECTURE	WINDOW	LINUX	UNIX
Ability to accommodate large number of concurrent users	6	7	9
Ability to accommodate large amount of stored data	7	7	8
Disaster recovery	7	5	8
EASE OF USE (OVERALL)	9	6	5
Ease of data access	10	9	9
Ease of administration	10	7	5
Flexibility	8	9	6
Initial architecture cost (hardware, O/S, RDBMS) to user	7	8	5
Number of third party applications available	7	5	9

CRITERIA/ ARCHITECTURE	WINDOW	LINUX	UNIX
Number of third party tools available (job schedulers, performance monitors, etc.)	6	6	8
PERFORMANCE (OVERALL)	4	7	9
Performance (Online Transaction Processing)	7	8	9
Performance (Decision Support)	6	7	9
RELIABILITY	7	7	9
Security	3	7	8
Scalability	7	7	9
Vendor Support	7	6	9

Venturing into the Great Unknown – New Database Architectures

If a new database architecture is selected (one that has never been used before) an additional set of concerns must be addressed:

- Venturing into new architectures will increase development time and training costs. Can the additional time and higher application development costs be justified?

- If the desired architecture requires support from the development area, can application personnel effectively administer the new architecture?

- Is the additional functionality or cost reduction the new architecture provides worth any additional risk to the application? This is often described as the *comfort ratio*.

- What is the business unit's, application area's and the IT department's vision of the future?

Conclusion

The database architecture (hardware platform and operating system) is the foundation for applications that run upon them. The most important decisions in the application development life cycle are the ones made during the initial stages of application design. The technologies to be used for data storage, data processing and application design and development are critical to the success of all application development projects. Even if your IT shop has experts in database administration and application design, their expertise will not overcome a poorly chosen or incorrectly designed architecture.

Each of the three architectures discussed is able to play a role in the IT infrastructure. It is important to choose the architecture that best meets the needs of the application being designed. Think about it, the foundation of anything is the most important part! Whether it is a bridge, a building or an application, everything built upon the foundation depends upon it. It is the most critical part of any complex creation. A well thought out, formalized and documented approach to the architecture selection process ensures that the selection process is not performed in a vacuum or based on personal preference. A part-time architecture team that is responsible for creating the architecture evaluation document and evaluating new applications fosters an intelligent approach to the architecture selection process.

In the next chapter, we'll discuss application design, testing and implementation, which are the next logical steps in the development process. The chapter will focus on application design review meetings that help to correct design and coding flaws as early as possible in the development process.

Review Meetings

CHAPTER 3

Oracle Database Design Review Meetings

One of the overlooked duties of an Oracle DBA is to inform, educate and assist the application development staff during the application development process. Although these responsibilities may not be formally assigned to the DBA, the DBA unit often finds that they are providing these services by default. The DBA is often considered to be a seasoned veteran who spends most of their time learning the subtle eccentricities of the Oracle database management system.

It is the DBA's responsibility to ensure that the overall design and implementation of the new application is proceeding according to expectations. Although application developers may be experts in SQL, procedural languages (Java, PL/SQL, C variations, etc.), they still turn to the DBA for help with standards, procedures, performance design, error recovery and complex SQL.

A continuous and effective dialogue between the DBA unit, system support personnel and application developers is of utmost importance throughout the entire application design and implementation process. One method to foster effective communications is for the DBA unit to create a series of new application design review meetings. These meetings can be organized in a manner that promotes efficient application usage of the

Oracle database environment. The design review meetings can be scheduled during logical break points between the different stages of the application development process.

The intent of this chapter is to help administrators design and standardize on a formalized design review process. The goal of the design review process is to identify and address application design, process flow, program logic and SQL statement problems early in the development lifecycle. Identifying these issues early in the development lifecycle allows them to be more easily addressed than if they were to be identified during later stages.

The database administration team should invite representatives from the development and business units to assist in the creation (and enforcement) of the standardized review process. Application development teams will be able to help tailor the design review process to satisfy their specific design and implementation needs. Business users who will be impacted by the production turnover will provide valuable input on implementing new applications for their specific business areas. Customized checklists are created to ensure that all application and business specific issues are addressed during each meeting of the design review process.

It is recommended that the database administration team then communicate to all application development and business areas that any internal applications created without following the standardized review process will not be migrated to production. Having the application teams and business units participate during the creation of the standardized review process allows the DBA team to enforce the policy without being viewed as dictatorial or making rules in a vacuum. In addition, every effort should be made to "sell" the standardized design review process in all communications to application development teams and business units.

The following list of meetings can be used as a starting point in the creation of a structured application design review process:

Initial Overview of Proposed System

The kickoff meeting is held with datacenter operations support managers, operating system administrators, application team leaders, system analysts, end-user management and data administrators to discuss the application's general purpose and function. This information will allow support technicians to determine the impact the new application will have on existing systems and allow them to begin planning the application design implementation process. The following information should be covered in this meeting:

- General description of purpose and function
- Application scope (enterprise wide application that affects all business units, intra-departmental that affects several business units or departmental)
- General application size (estimated number of programs, data objects)
- Criticalness of the application (mission critical, application critical, non-critical)

- Application availability requirements and downtime windows
- Application type (decision support, business intelligence, data warehouse, data mart, online transaction processing)
- Architecture design (web server, application server, N-tier, distributed database environment)
- Advanced features required (replication, advanced queuing)
- Data feeds required from other architectures
- Load processing
- Batch processing
- Online transaction processing
- Development tools used to build front-end application screens
- Third-party tools used to provide Ad-Hoc query access
- Procedural language used to build business logic (Java, PL/SQL)
- Application development methodology to be used (JAD, RAD)
- Number of concurrent users
- Disk storage and data growth estimates
- Highly available architecture discussion (RAC, Oracle Fail Safe, Data Guard, hardware vendor clustering and failover)
- Performance expectations
- Criteria used to judge performance

- Security and auditing requirements
- Hardware platform, O/S preferences/selection and sizing discussion
- Hardware platform, O/S installation, operation and administration
- Division of duties between the DBA, application development and business units

Logical Data Model Review

This meeting is convened as soon as the logical data model is complete. The major emphasis of this meeting is to determine if the logical data model is complete and correct. The application's process model (if one is available) can also be verified at this time. Volume statistics, object growth rates, purge criteria, referential integrity needs and application-naming conventions are also discussed. Knowing your data before hand is essential to designing processes to manipulate that data. The following topics are covered in this meeting:

- Determine if the data model is fully documented (entities, attributes, relationships)
- Attributes have correct datatype, length, NULL status, default values
- General discussion of business rules that are to be enforced by database level constraints
    - Not null constraints
    - Check constraints
    - Unique constraints
    - Primary key constraints

- - o Foreign key constraints
- Business rules to be enforced by triggers and procedures
- Business rules to be enforced by application code
- Logical/process model comparison
- Volume statistics
- Growth rates and purge criteria

Designing for Performance

This meeting is held with the application development units before any physical DDL is generated by the DBA. Proper transaction design and efficient SQL coding results in less performance-oriented database alterations being made during the latter stages of the design and implementation process. Determining predicate usage will allow the DBA to create additional database objects (indexes, materialized views, index organized tables) to increase SQL, and subsequently, application performance. The following information is discussed:

- Normalization vs denormalization
- Table access requirements and predicate usage
- Database objects used to increase SQL performance including:
  - o B-Tree Indexes
  - o Bitmap Indexes
  - o Bitmap join indexes
  - o Function-Based indexes
  - o Materialized views

- - Index organized tables
    - External tables
  - Data partitioning algorithms
    - Range partitioning
    - Hash partitioning
    - List partitioning
    - Composite partitioning
  - Process parallelism (parallel query, parallel DML, parallel load)
  - Transaction modeling
  - Oracle SQL performance features
    - Full table scan vs index access
    - Hash joins
    - Star joins
    - Index skip scans
    - Index fast full scans
    - Cursor sharing (SQL statement reuse and soft parse vs hard parse)
    - Bind variables
  - Reinforcement of effective SQL coding techniques

Setting up a Successful Test System in Oracle

This meeting is held as soon as the application developers are ready to begin the actual coding process. The ultimate goal of this meeting is for application developers to have a firm understanding of what is required to create and maintain a successful Oracle test environment. Discussions on Oracle utilities, SQL statements, procedural code, Oracle security, batch script testing, benchmarking, testing and monitoring are of prime importance at this time. The DBA must make it clear to all involved that the DBA unit is always available to answer questions and troubleshoot poorly performing SQL throughout the entire application development life cycle. It is imperative that the DBA make every effort to find and correct problems during this stage of the development process. Maintaining a proactive stance instead of a reactive one will always prove to be beneficial when it comes to correcting design problems. There are always enough potential problems lurking in the system for the DBA to solve without adding any additional ones through faulty application design. Topics to be discussed in this meeting include:

- Division of duties between DBA, systems, application development and business units
- Test hardware platform, O/S installation, configuration and administration
- Data feeds required from other architectures
- Data load and update processing and scheduling
- SQL Loader control cards
- Test system availability requirements
- Test system backup and recovery requirements
- Oracle security authorization
- Tools to aid in application development
- Oracle Enterprise Manager toolset

- In-house monitoring tools
- Third-party vendor products
- Benchmarking and performance measurements

Monitoring Performance During Testing

Because this meeting and the previously discussed Setting Up a Successful Test System are closely related, they may be discussed together to save time and provide greater clarity. The DBA and developers need to have an understanding of what information is required to effectively monitor the performance of the Oracle application throughout the entire testing process. The DBA can offer to show developers how to use the various toolsets provided by Oracle (Oracle Enterprise Manager, SQL Trace, explain plan, BSTAT/ESTAT, autotrace, Oracle traces, V$ tables and Statspack) so that developers can play an active role in performance measurement. Suggested discussion topics are as follows:

- Names of all SQL Loader control cards and batch scripts
- Performance measurement goals and expectations
- Determine the test load volume (data volume, concurrent users) required to accurately predict production performance
- Comparison of test system load to estimated production load
- Oracle performance measurement tools. Suggested tools include:
    - Explain

- o SQL*Plus autotrace
- o Oracle SQL trace
- o Statspack
- o Oracle Enterprise Manager with Tuning Pack option
- o V$ performance tables
- Index utilization monitoring via ALTER INDEX MONITORING statement
- Third party performance monitoring tools
- LAN performance monitoring tools
- Operating system performance monitoring tools

Performance Design Reviews

Information collected from the various performance monitoring tools is discussed at this time. One meeting may be sufficient, but large application development efforts usually require several discussions. If the DBA has maintained good communications throughout the initial stages of application design, there should be few surprises when these meetings are held. SQL tuning and tweaking recommendations are covered in this meeting. Depending on the length of the development process, follow-up meetings can be held to ensure that the application is performing as expected. Some suggested topics include:

- Load testing assessment. Is the load being placed on the test system large enough to accurately predict production performance?

- Review performance statistics collected during the testing process
- Assess SQL coding techniques by reviewing explain plan output for performance critical transactions
    - Index usage
    - Local/join predicates
    - Join methods
    - Subselects
    - View materialization
- Determine if additional Oracle objects need to be created to enhance SQL performance
    - B-Tree Indexes
    - Bitmap Indexes
    - Bitmap join indexes
    - Function-Based indexes
    - Materialized views
    - Index organized tables
    - External tables

Preparation for Production Turnover

This meeting is held to determine if there are any last minute questions and to make certain that everyone knows what is expected of them during the final turnover process. All units that have participated in the application design or application design review process are invited to attend. To ensure that all steps necessary for a successful migration to production are executed, the use of a standardized Oracle migration checklist is highly recommended. This document will allow the DBAs and developers to concern themselves with topics that are related to this specific turnover rather than spending time on the more mundane turnover tasks that are just as important, but easily forgotten. Having a complete, well thought-out migration checklist produces a less stressful and less error prone production migration process. Topics include:

- Division of duties between DBA, systems, application development and business units
- Production hardware platform, O/S installation, configuration and operation
- Data feeds required from other architectures
- Data load and update processing and scheduling
- SQL Loader control cards
- Backup and recovery
- Oracle security authorization
- DBA forms and turnover procedures
- Contact information and escalation procedures
- Post production monitoring tools to be used

Post Production Turnover

This final set of meetings is held after the production turnover is complete. Application logic errors and performance problem resolution are the prime topics of discussion. A comparison of the actual performance to the anticipated performance of the application is also discussed. The review and correction process, by its nature, is iterative. The problems are identified, a plan of attack to solve them is agreed upon and additional meetings are scheduled to review the results. As additional problems are identified, they are added to the list of problems to be solved. This iterative process continues until all major performance issues and application logic errors are addressed. The post production turnover meetings should include discussions on:

- Review performance statistics collected (Oracle Enterprise Manager, SQL Trace, explain plan, BSTAT/ESTAT, autotrace, Oracle traces, V$ tables and Statspack)
- Assess SQL coding techniques by reviewing explain plan output for transactions experiencing performance problems
    - Index usage
    - Local/join predicates
    - Join methods
    - Subselects
    - View materialization
- Determine if additional Oracle objects need to be created to enhance SQL performance
    - B-Tree Indexes
    - Bitmap Indexes
    - Bitmap join indexes
    - Function-Based indexes
    - Materialized views

- o Index organized tables
- o External tables

Oracle Database Design Review Meetings – Conclusion

These recommendations are not intended to coerce readers into using the Oracle application design review meeting examples verbatim but to emphasize the importance of a structured approach to the design review process. The seemingly endless combinations of application architectures and software products used for application development may require the creation of a fully customized design review process for each application development project. The overall goal of design review meetings is to ensure the involvement of technical support units during the application's design and implementation. When Oracle design issues are addressed early in the development lifecycle, problems are minimized and the migration from test to production is more easily accomplished.

Conclusion

The overall intent of the design review meetings is to identify and correct design and coding flaws as early as possible in the development process. It's based on a simple premise - the earlier the problems are caught, the easier they are to fix.

Hopefully this chapter persuaded readers to pursue a structured approach to the design review process. The suggestions contained in this chapter can be used as the basis for a customized design review checklist that meets your organization's specific business and technical requirements.

The next chapter will provide readers with the general principles of database administration. It begins with database installation and ends with a discussion on Oracle memory structures. The chapter also attempts to answer a few of the most often asked questions from students in my Oracle classes.

Oracle Database Administration

CHAPTER 4

We finally begin our discussion of Oracle database administration. In this next section, we will cover database administration techniques, tips and tricks. Along the way we'll also learn how Oracle works.

Oracle Software Installation

In the past, installing Oracle used to be "a pain." Describing it as "a pain" is like saying the Titanic had a small leak. Installations used to take hours and problems were commonplace. The Java-enabled installer program made the installer much easier to use and as the installer matured, performance increased and the number of installation problems decreased.

The most important thing to remember is to use the manual as a cookbook. Follow the steps that Oracle recommends and DO NOT DEVIATE from them. The installation guide is your friend and if you don't understand some of the operating system commands provided in the manual, make friends with your local O/S administrator.

Some of the more common problems are:

- Insufficient disk space – Check the installation guide before you start the install. If you are going to create a starter database during the install, make sure you have enough disk space available. Oracle9i requires up to 3.5 GIGs of disk space for the binaries alone. Some windows installations may have a slightly smaller footprint, but not by much. For UNIX systems, the Oracle Universal Installer requires up to 400 MB of space in the /tmp directory.

During our beta-test of Oracle9i, we created a database during the install and specified that all files would be Oracle managed (discussed later) using the default file size specifications. The end result was a 1 GIG database. The default file size specification for Oracle managed files is 100 MEGs. The starter database consisted of a 100 MEG system, users, undo, temp and three groups of redo logs with both members being 100MEG in size.

- Improper permissions – The installation guide details the security permissions required to do a successful install.
- UNIX/LINUX – Shared memory and semaphore parameters. The system configuration file (/etc/system in the many UNIX systems) contains parameters used to configure shared memory parameters and semaphores.

Migrating to Newer Oracle Releases

One of the tasks that make many DBAs lie awake nights is the database upgrade. Most point upgrades (i.e. 8.1.6 to 8.1.7) are relatively simple. The DBA runs a few SQL scripts to upgrade the database to the new release. Because they are more complicated and error-prone, let's focus our attention on major database upgrades (i.e. Oracle 8i to Oracle9i).

The following tips will help:

- Read the migration manual and follow it like a cookbook.

- Hope for the best but prepare for the worst-case scenario. When reading the migration manual, pay special attention to the common migration problems and back-off procedure sections.

- Create a migration document that includes checklists, application test plans, back-off procedures and business user contacts. Include a step-by-step description of the activities that will be executed during the migration process. Contact information for everyone involved in the migration should also be included in the migration document.

- Perform the upgrade in test and ask the developers to run a complete test of the applications that access the database being upgraded.

- Create application developer and business user sign off documents. Once the developers and business users have completed their testing, the documents will be signed and the initial migration process will be complete.

- Schedule a meeting with operating system administrators, application developers, operations personnel and business users to discuss the migration process. Discuss and verify the contents of the turnover document. This meeting will also ensure that everyone understands what is expected of him or her during the migration process.

- A cold database backup of all datafiles, control files, redo logs, parameter file and password file will provide the foundation for successful database restoration.

The migration manual provides the DBA with several different methods to perform the upgrade. Let's take a quick look at two of the more common alternatives:

- **Migration Utility** – The migration utility has matured over time to where it has become one of the preferred methods of performing database upgrades The utility walks the DBA through the migration process which reduces the possibility of user error. Because the utility does not require additional disk space to perform the migration, databases of any size can be easily migrated. One of the drawbacks is that the DBA is unable to move the database to a new server or operating system while performing the migration.

- **Export/Import** – Using Export/Import to perform database upgrades can be described as follows: the utility has been around forever (I have been using it since Version 6), it is very reliable and it is very, very slow. Export/Import is often the only method that allows the DBA to migrate databases from very old releases to more current versions. The DBA uses the Export utility to migrate the database data to a flat file from the old release and uses the Import to load the data into the database created using the new release's binaries. Export/Import is not the preferred method of upgrading large databases due to its slow performance and additional disk space requirements for the Export's output files and duplicate database data files. Since the database is duplicated, switching back to the old release is simple and straightforward. Unlike its migration utility counterpart, Export/Import can be used to move the database to a new server or operating system during the migration process. One last thing to consider, the Import may set the status column of stored PL/SQL programs and views in DBA_OBJECTS to 'INVALID'. Have a script ready that recompiles all invalid stored PL/SQL programs to validate them. Because of object dependencies, you may have to run the script several times before all invalid objects successfully recompiled.

The Oracle Database Fundamentals I (1Z0-031) certification test will have a few questions on the Oracle Export and Import utilities. Test candidates should have an understanding of the following:

- Basic architecture of the Export and Import
- Control parameters used as input to both utilities
- The differences between a conventional Export and a direct Export
- The order in which Import creates the Oracle objects (i.e. tables, indexes, referential integrity, bitmap indexes)
- There always seems to be a question or two on the IGNORE=Y parameter

UNIX and LINUX Semaphores and Shared Memory

What exactly are shared memory parameters and semaphores? The information below should help.

Semaphores

A detailed definition from Oracle's support site states "Semaphores are integer-valued objects set aside by the operating system that can be incremented or decremented atomically. They are designed to allow processes to synchronize execution, by only allowing one process to perform an operation on the semaphore at a time. The other process(es) sleep until the semaphores values are either incremented or set to 0, depending on the options used. Semaphores are generally not used one at a time, so Unix uses the concept of semaphore sets to make it easier to allocate and refer to semaphores. When your Unix kernel is configured, the maximum number of semaphores that will be available to the system is set. Also set is the maximum number of semaphores per set, and the maximum number of sets that can be allocated."

These small, memory storage areas are used by Oracle to control concurrency and communications between the various background processes (PMON, SMON, DBWR, LGWR, etc.). Semaphores make sure that the background processes "talk" to each other in a coordinated fashion. Equate the Oracle instance to a meeting with many participants. If everyone talked at once, nobody would understand anything and nothing would be accomplished. The semaphore is like the meeting leader who only allows selected participants to talk to each other at the same time. In addition, semaphores are the air traffic controllers of a UNIX system. When a process needs access to a particular component that is not available, the semaphore places the requesting process into a holding pattern. Semaphores make sure that the Oracle background processes perform their tasks at the right time and that two processes that shouldn't work together, don't.

In many systems, administrators can find out how many semaphores are currently allocated by typing "*ipcs -sb*" at the operating system prompt. The output will display the semaphore sets allocated, their identifying number, the owner and the number of semaphores in each set.

Oracle allocates semaphores for background processes during instance start. The *init.ora* parameter "processes" is used by Oracle to determine how many additional semaphores will be allocated during the startup process. Remember that Oracle allocates all semaphores during the startup process, whether they are all needed or not.

Semaphore allocation errors are caused by insufficient system settings, a high value in the *init.ora* PROCESSES parameter or failed processes not releasing previously allocated semaphores and semaphore sets. Because each Oracle instance reserves its own semaphores at startup, multiple instance environments require more semaphore allocations than their single instance counterparts.

The system file parameters that govern semaphore allocation during startup are:

- *semmns* - The number of semaphores in the system.

- *semmni* - The number of semaphore set identifiers in the system; determines the number of semaphore sets that can be created at any one time.

- *semmsl* - The maximum number of semaphores that can be in one semaphore set. It should be same size as maximum number of Oracle processes.

The Oracle installation guides provide recommended settings for the values above. If you do not have enough free semaphores available, expect one (or more) of the following error messages during Oracle instance startup:

- ORA-7250 "spcre: semget error, unable to get first semaphore set."

- ORA-7279 "spcre: semget error, unable to get first semaphore set."

- ORA-7251 "spcre: semget error, could not allocate any semaphores."

- ORA-7252 "spcre: semget error, could not allocate any semaphores."

- ORA-7339 "spcre: maximum number of semaphore sets exceeded."

Administrators can correct these errors by:

- Using the "*ipcs -sb*" command to determine if any dead process are still allocating semaphores.

- Configuring more semaphores on the system.

- Reducing the value of the PROCESSES *init.ora* parameter. This may require reducing the processes parameter for multiple instances in multiple instance environments.

Shared Memory

Processes running in UNIX and LINUX often use shared memory regions to perform their work. The Oracle SGA is a good example. It is a common area of memory that is concurrently shared by many different processes. The SGA must be accessible to all database sessions for the instance to function.

The operating system parameter *shmmax* (Shared Memory Maximum) determines how large of a shared memory segment region can be allocated by an application. The application may not be able to allocate a contiguous chunk of memory from the operating system. If sufficient memory is available (but not contiguous) the application may be granted access to the shared memory in multiple segments.

The system file parameters that govern shared memory allocation during startup are:

- *shmmax* - The maximum size(in bytes) of a single shared memory segment.

- *shmmin* - The minimum size(in bytes) of a single shared memory segment.

- *shmmni* - The number of shared memory identifiers.

- *shmseg* - The maximum number of shared memory segments that can be attached by a process.

Like semaphores, the Oracle installation guides provide recommended settings for the values above. The size of a single Oracle SGA cannot exceed the value in SHMMAX. The following messages may occur when attempting to allocate a SGA that is larger than the allowable shared memory segment or insufficient memory is available:

- ORA-27100 "shared memory realm already exists"
- ORA-27102 "out of memory"
- ORA-27125 "unable to create shared memory segment" or "linux 43 identifier removed"
- ORA-27123 "unable to attach to shared memory segment"

Administrators can correct the above error messages by:

- Reducing parameter values that control SGA size. Unlike semaphores, these values are not cumulative in nature. The size of a single SGA cannot be larger than the *shmmax* value but multiple SGAs can be.
- Increasing the value for *shmmax*.
- Adding memory to the hardware platform.

Relinking Oracle8i and Oracle9i Products

Oracle8.0 and previous releases provide two different ways to relink Oracle:

- Using the MAKE command and specifying the MAKE files for a particular product.
- Using the Oracle installer and relinking from the administrative task menu.

Oracle 8.1.5 continued to provide support for the MAKE command but the Oracle Universal Installer no longer included an option to perform product relinks. Oracle 8.1.5 introduced a more user-friendly tool to relink the Oracle products. The RELINK shell script in

$ORACLE_HOME/bin can be used with the following parameters to relink the Oracle executables:

- ALL -- everything which has been installed
- ORACLE -- oracle database executable only
- NETWORK -- *net_client, net_server, cman, cnames*
- CLIENT -- *net_client, otrace, plsql*
- CLIENT_SHAREDLIB - *interMedia ctx, ordimg, ordaud, ordvir, md*
- PRECOMP -- all precompilers which have been installed
- UTILITIES -- utilities
- OEMAGENT -- *oemagent, odg*

Windows Services

Since our most recent discussion centered on UNIX and LINUX, let's give Microsoft Windows equal time by turning our attention to Oracle Services on Windows platforms. Those of us who have administered Oracle on Windows are aware that a service is required for each instance that runs in a Widows environment. Services are required because they are the only way in Windows environments to start a process without having a user connected.

Administrators use the database creation assistant (DBCA) or ORADIM utility to create the service prior to creating the database. The service must be started before the database can be accessed. Although the instance can be started and stopped independently using the STARTUP and SHUTDOWN commands, the database is stopped when the service is stopped and started when the service is started.

One of the specifications supplied to DBCA and ORADIM is the *–pfile* parameter. It identifies where the service will look to find the parameter file during instance startup. If it doesn't match the Oracle default directory ($ORACLE_HOME\database) you will have to use the parameter override statement when using SQL*PLUS or SVRMGRL to start the database manually. Remember, if you move the parameter or SPFILE to a different location, you will have to use the –EDIT option of the ORADIM utility to change where the service looks for the parameter file.

A neat trick to get around this problem is to create a parameter file in the default location that points to the PFILE or SPFILE (whichever one you are using). The entry in the PFILE would look like:

```
SPFILE = /database/startup/spfilexxxxx.ora   OR
IFILE = /database/startup/initxxxxx.ora
```

Where xxxx is your instance name.

Oracle Instance Administration

An Oracle instance consists of a combination of all of the memory structures and database background processes that are allocated during database start. Care should be taken to use the proper terminology when discussing the Oracle server. Oracle differentiates between an Oracle instance and an Oracle database. Oracle support personnel do not use the terms interchangeably. The following few sections provide a few hints and tips on Oracle instance administration.

Oracle9i Persistent Initialization Parameter Files

Oracle9i introduces on-line parameter changes that persist across database shutdowns and startups. This feature allows administrators to make changes to database initialization parameters and have them take affect immediately. In the past, these changes would require the administrator to edit the database's parameter file (*initsid.ora*). Because Oracle only reads the parameter file during startup, the changes would not take affect until the next time the database was shutdown and restarted.

In Oracle9I, a server-based parameter file, called a SPFILE, is used as the repository for initialization parameters. Oracle9i documentation now refers to the old *initsid.ora* parameter file as the PFILE. The SPFILE is initially created by using the PFILE (*initsid.ora*) parameter file as the source. It is important to note that the database is initially created using the old PFILE parameter file. Administrators then use the "CREATE SPFILE FROM PFILE" command to create the server-based parameter file. At system startup, the default behavior of the STARTUP command is to look for the SPFILE before it looks for the PFILE. The Oracle administration guides provide information on default location and naming conventions for server-based parameter files.

The administrator uses the ALTER SYSTEM statement to dynamically change initialization parameters. A parameter can be changed immediately or deferred until the next database startup. Although the majority of the parameters can be dynamically changed, there are a few configuration parameters that can only be changed by editing the old *initsid.ora* parameter file (PFILE). Here are a few hints on PFILEs and SPFILEs:

- Never, ever edit a SPFILE manually. Although you can view it in both UNIX and Windows editors, editing it can produce a "less than desirable" outcome. The SPFILE was edited three times during our beta testing and the result was three database recreates.

- If you are required to edit the PFILE to change a static parameter, don't forget to execute the 'CREATE PFILE FROM SPFILE' statement to refresh the PFILE with all of the dynamic changes recorded in the SPFILE. Do the SPFILE to PFILE refresh before you edit the PFILE. If you don't, you could lose the dynamic changes recorded in the SPFILE. Remember, the database looks for the SPFILE first during startup, so you will need to execute the "CREATE SPFILE FROM PFILE" (after you edit the PFILE) to migrate your changes. If your PFILE doesn't have a record of all your dynamic parameter changes, you will lose them when you execute the 'CREATE PFILE FROM SPFILE' statement. The recommended procedure is to always execute the 'CREATE PFILE FROM SPFILE' command after dynamically changing a parameter to back up the changes recorded in the SPFILE to the PFILE.

Oracle9i Persistent Initialization Parameter Files

Oracel9i provides a new static parameter called *max_sga_size* that specifies the maximum size of SGA for the lifetime of the instance. Another new Oracle9i parameter *db_cache_size* replaces *db_block_buffers*. *db_block_buffers* is still provided for backwards compatibility. *db_block_buffers* and the *max_sga_size* parameters are static so they can only be changed by editing the PFILE, then executing the 'CREATE SPFILE FROM PFILE' statement and restarting the instance.

During our testing, we found that the online changes to parameters worked well. We did find that changing SGA parameters produced some interesting results. We were able to dynamically alter the initialization parameters that affect the size of the buffer caches, shared pool, and large pool, but only to the extent that the sum of these sizes and the sizes of the other components of the SGA (fixed SGA, variable SGA, and redo log buffers) did not exceed the value specified by *sga_max_size*. Oracle also never really released the memory back to the operating system. When the data buffer cache was reduced the shared pool size would increase by the amount of the data buffer cache reduction. The same event occurred when we reduced the shared pool size, the data buffer cache would be increased by the amount of memory that was removed from the shared pool.

Oracle recommends that you execute the 'CREATE PFILE FROM SPFILE' statement on a regular basis. This backs up the SPFILE to the PFILE. Administrators must have the SYSDBA or the SYSOPER system privilege to execute this statement. The PFILE is created on the database server machine in the default location. Administrators are able to overide the PFILE name and location by fully qualifying the PFILE parameter (CREATE PFILE= '/u01/oradata/orcl/test_initorcl.ora' FROM SPFILE').

If the SPFILE is missing or corrupt, administrators can start up the instance using the PFILE. Oracle looks for the initialization parameter file in the default location by examining filenames in the following order:

- spfile$ORACLE_SID.ora
- spfile.ora
- init$ORACLE_SID.ora

If the SPFILE becomes corrupt, delete the SPFILE and Oracle will use the backup PFILE (*init$ORACLE_SID.ora*).

The Oracle Database Fundamentals I (1Z0-031) certification test will contain a few questions on Persistent Initialization Parameter Files. The questions will cover the following topics:

- The differences between the SPFILE and the PFILE
- The order in which the SPFILE and PFILE are read
- The default location of the SPFILE
- Editing the SPFILE manually
- A few questions on the use of the SCOPE parameter used in the ALTER SYSTEM SET……. Command

Remote Startup/Shutdown

Oracle9i's persistent parameter files provide administrators with the ability to start an Oracle instance using SQL*Plus on remote clients.

Before we begin, some background information is in order. Oracle has been promising to desupport server manager and CONNECT INTERNAL for some time now. Administrators would use server manager on the host to connect to the database using the INTERNAL account to start and stop an Oracle instance.

Server manager and CONNECT INTERNAL are officially desupported in Oracle9i and are replaced by SQL*Plus and a special privilege called SYSDBA. SQL*Plus and SYSDBA have been available for some time but were never a primary means of starting and stopping an Oracle instance.

During an instance start, Oracle reads instance configuration parameters from a SPFILE or PFILE. In order to facilitate remote startup and shutdown, SQL*Plus is now able to reference the server-based parameter file (SPFILE) from remote clients. This solves the problem of propagating copies of the PFILE to all remote clients that require the ability to start an Oracle instance. By having all clients point to a single source, administrators can rest easy knowing the same parameters are used to configure the instance during each startup.

The steps to access a SPFILE from a remote client are as follows:

1. A server-based parameter file (SPFILE) is configured on the database server by executing the 'CREATE SPFILE FROM PFILE' command.

2. Create a parameter file on the remote client that contains a single line that references the server-based SPFILE:

   ```
   spfile=/u01/app/oracle/product/9.0.0/dbs/spfiledemo1.ora
   ```

3. Start SQL*Plus without connecting to the database by executing:

   ```
   SQL*PLUS /nolog
   ```

4. Connect to the remote instance as SYSDBA:

   ```
   CONNECT username/password@connect_identifier AS SYSDBA
   ```

5. Start the instance by executing:

   ```
   STARTUP PFILE=pfilename.ora
   * where pfilename.ora is the parameter file name created in
   step 2.
   ```

Standard operating practice in UNIX environments is to embed STARTUP and SHUTDOWN commands in server manager to start and stop an Oracle instance. Shops migrating existing databases to Oracle9i should change the scripts from server manager to SQL*PLUS.

Multiple Buffer Pools

Oracle8 introduced a new paradigm for managing buffer pools. Database administrators are no longer forced to use a single buffer pool to store application data. Multiple buffer pools allow administers to divide schema objects (tables, indexes and clusters) into different data buffers. Oracle allows you to configure keep and recycle buffer pools to tailor the data buffers to meet application requirements.

- Default Buffer Pool - The default buffer pool is equivalent to using a single buffer cache. The default buffer pool always exists and the size of the default buffer pool is not explicitly defined. The size of the default buffer pool depends on the amount of data buffers remaining after the keep and recycle buffer pools have been allocated. Objects that are defined without a buffer pool specified will use the default buffer pool.

- Keep Buffer Pool - As the name suggests, the goal of the keep buffer pool is to retain objects in memory. The size of the keep buffer pool will depend on the objects the DBA wants to keep in the buffer cache.

- Recycle Buffer Pool - The recycle buffer pool tries to eliminate blocks from memory as soon as they are no longer needed. If the recycle buffer pool is too small, transactions accessing the same block multiple times may find that the block has aged out before it has completed processing. If the block is flushed from the cache before the transaction is complete, the transaction must read from disk again to retrieve the block's contents.

The recycle buffer pool can be used to prevent objects from dominating the keep or default buffer pools. Tables that are accessed by table scans, large segments accessed by random reads and non-performance critical tables and indexes are all good candidates for the recycle buffer pool.

Specifying Default, Keep and Recycle Bufferpools in Oracle8 and Oracle8i

You define each buffer pool using the *buffer_pool_name init.ora* parameter. The name can be DEFAULT, KEEP or RECYCLE. You specify two attributes for each buffer pool: the number of buffers in the buffer pool and the number of LRU latches allocated to the buffer pool. The *db_block_buffers* parameter is now used to define the total number of buffers available to the database instance. The keep and recycle buffer pools are created from this total amount with the remainder allocated to the default buffer pool. If the number of buffers allocated to the user defined buffer pools exceeds the total specified by *db_block_buffers*, an error occurs and the database is not mounted.

The Oracle Database Fundamentals I (1Z0-031) and the Oracle Database Performance Tuning (1Z0-033) certification tests will always have a few questions on the different bufferpools. Test candidates should know the following information:

- The differences between the Default, Keep and Recycle bufferpools
- How to allocate memory to the different bufferpools
- When to use the Default,.Keep and Recycle bufferpools

Specifying Default, Keep and Recycle Bufferpools in Oracle9i

buffer_pool_keep and *buffer_pool_recycle* are no longer recommended in Oracle9i and are retained for backward compatibility. *buffer_pool_keep* and *buffer_pool_recycle* cannot be combined with the new Oracle9i dynamic parameters *db_keep_cache_size* and *db_recycle_cache_size*. Oracle recommends using *db_keep_cache_size* and *db_recycle_cache_size* to specify keep and recycle buffer pools in Oracle9i.

Large Pool

The shared pool region of the SGA consists of several, smaller memory components. These individual memory components are sized by a single parameter (*shared_pool_size*). The shared pool allocates memory for the library cache, the data dictionary cache and session information for systems that are using Oracle's multithreaded server (renamed to Shared Server in Oracle9i). As a result, the shared pool is often the second largest component of the SGA.

The multithreaded server also uses the shared pool for user sorting operations on row data requested by CREATE INDEX, SQL ORDER BY, SQL GROUP BY and table join methods. If the instance does not use multithreaded server, the *sort_area_size* parameter in Oracle8i and the *pga_aggregate_target* parameter in Oracle9i is used to allocate memory for each session that requests memory for sorting. Problems begin to occur for multithreaded instances that require user sort operations to be performed. These user sort operations begin to dominate the shared pool memory area. Oracle8 introduced the *large_pool_size* parameter to offer administrators the capability of creating a memory storage area for the exclusive use of user sort operations in multithreaded server environments. This removes the conflicts that occur between user sort operations and library and data dictionary cache requests.

The large pool allocation is used in multithreaded environments for session memory, by parallel execution for message buffers, and by RMAN backup processes for disk I/O buffers. Parallel execution allocates buffers out of the large pool only when *parallel_automatic_tuning* is set to true.

Java Pool

The Oracle9i Concepts manual describes the java pool as " memory in the SGA reserved for session-specific Java code and data within the JVM. This memory includes the shared in-memory representation of Java method and class definitions, as well as the Java objects that are migrated to the Java session space at end-of-call." The *init.ora* parameter *java_pool_size* specifies the size (in bytes) of the Java pool. The default value for *java_pool_size* is 20 MEGs.

If your application does not use Java and you reduce the size of the Java pool to free up resources, it may cause problems with the Oracle Export utility. If you lower the Java Pool size and begin experiencing ORA-4031 (out of memory) errors, increase the size of the Java pool to its default size of 20M. This is a common problem in Oracle 8.1.x installations.

Redo log Buffer Performance

The following query returns the number of redo log space requests that have occurred since instance startup:

```
SELECT substr(name,1,30), value FROM v$sysstat WHERE name =
'redo log space requests';
```

Redo log space requests is the number of times a user process waits for space in the redo log buffer. The number should be close to 0. If it is not, increase the size of the *log_buffer* parameter.

Buffer Performance is critical to Good Oracle Performance

Make sure enough memory is allocated to the data buffer cache, the shared pool, and the log buffers. Their order of importance and hit ratios are:

- Shared pool (mainly because it contains the library cache) – the hit ratio should be 98% or higher
- Data buffer cache – the hit ratio should be 95% or higher
- Log buffer – keep redo log space requests to a minimum

All of the Oracle certification tests will have numerous questions on the memory areas used by an Oracle database. Test candidates should have a firm understanding of:

- How the different memory areas are used by Oracle
    o Large Pool
    o Java pool

- o Shared pool
- How an Oracle Shared Server Environment uses the shared pool vs. how it is used by a Dedicated Server
- The differences between the library cache and the data dictionary cache
- The differences between a hard parse and a soft parse
  - o Data Buffer Cache
    - The difference between the *db_block_buffers* and the *db_cache_size* parameters
  - o Log Buffer
  - o PGA
- The parameters used in the parameter file to size the various memory areas. The test always seems to have a few questions on how to size the different data buffer caches including the Default, Keep and Recycle caches and non-standard blocksize caches (2K, 4K, 8K, etc.)
- Dynamic SGA sizing including a question on the *sga_max_size* parameter

DBWR_IO_SLAVES vs DB_WRITER_PROCESSES

Questions about multiple DBWR processes have plagued DBAs since Oracle7. You configured multiple DBWR process in Oracle7 by setting the parameter DB_WRITERS. In Oracle7, multiple DBWR processes were actually slave processes that were unable to perform asynchronous I/O calls on their own. The algorithm used by the Oracle7 DBWR caused it to incur waits when the delay of a single write caused additional writes to queue up until the initial write was complete.

Oracle8 and later release's DBWR architecture corrects this problem. Oracle's DBWR now writes continuously without waiting for previous writes to complete. The new design allows DBWR to act as if it were inherently synchronous, regardless of whether the operating system supports asynchronous I/O or not. Administrators are able to configure multiple DBWR process by setting the *init.ora* parameter *db_writer_processes*. Multiple database writers became available in Oracle 8.0.4 and allow true multiple database writes. There is no master-slave relationship as in Version 7.

If you implement database writer I/O slaves by setting the *dbwr_io_slaves* parameter, you configure a single (master) DBWR process that has slave processes that are subservient to perform asynchronous I/O calls. I/O slaves can also be used to simulate asynchronous I/O on platforms that do not support asynchronous I/O or implement it inefficiently.

You can't activate both multiple DBWRs and I/O slaves. If both parameters are set in the parameter file, *dbwr_io_slaves* will take precedence.

To determine whether to use multiple DBWn processes or database slaves, follow these guidelines:
- Use *db_writer_processes* for most write intensive applications. One per CPU is the recommended setting.

- Use *db_writer_processes* for databases that have a large data buffer cache.

- Use *dbwr_io_slaves* for applications that are not write intensive and run on operating systems that support asynchronous I/O.

- Use *dbwr_io_slaves* on platforms that do no support asynchronous I/O.

- Use *dbwr_io_slaves* on single CPU systems. Multiple DBWR processes are CPU intensive.

Conclusion

This chapter covered a lot of different topics. From installing and upgrading the database to Oracle internals and memory structures. The key points to remember from this chapter are:

- Follow the upgrade and installation guides like a cookbook. You should only deviate from them when it is absolutely required.

- The UNIX and LINUX environments require some additional kernel parameter settings (semaphores and shared memory segments) that although often overlooked, are critical to a trouble-free Oracle database environment.

- Use the ORADIM utility to create the Oracle Windows service, which is required on all Windows platforms.

- Oracle9i provides administrators with a new parameter file, called the SPFILE that allows the database to be configured dynamically. Changes made in the SPFILE are also persistent which means the changes remain in effect after the database has been recycled.

- Never, ever edit the SPFILE.
- As I tell all of my entry-level classes "memory FAST, disk SLOW". Start your database tuning process by looking at the hit ratios for the shared pool and database buffer cache.

Our next chapter will cover Oracle database objects. The chapter begins by providing information database objects (control files, redo logs, tablespaces, datafiles. rollback segments) and finishes with a discussion on Oracle tables and indexes.

Oracle Database Objects

CHAPTER 5

The following sections provide some interesting information on Oracle database objects (tablespaces, tables, indexes). To keep the reading lively, I'll intersperse some tuning information and hints, tips and tricks in the discussion. This section is not an all-encompassing guide to administering Oracle objects, rather it is a collection of information that I felt that was important to all DBAs, regardless of the experience level.

What Database Are You Working In?

Working in the wrong database is a common problem for database experts as well as their less experienced counterparts. How many times have YOU found yourself running statements in the wrong environment? Feel free to include me in that not so select group. The operating system command SET can be used in Windows systems to display environment variables. The ENV command can be used to display the environment variables in UNIX. Many seasoned database administrators change their UNIX shell prompt in their.profile to display the current Oracle SID. Displaying the current Oracle SID in the shell's prompt provides a continuous reminder to the DBA of the database they are working in.

GLOGIN.SQL and LOGIN.SQL

Administrators are able to use two configuration files, *glogin.sql* and *login.sql* to customize their SQL*PLUS environment (including the prompt). When a user activates SQL*PLUS and connects to the database, SQL*PLUS will execute the contents of the *glogin.sql* configuration file in $ORACLE_HOME/sqlplus/admin.

After the *glogin.sql* file has been executed, SQL*PLUS will execute *login.sql*. Oracle will look for the *login.sql* file in the current working directory (where you started SQL*PLUS) and the operating system environment variable *sqlpath*. Remember that the statements in the *login.sql* file take precedence over *glogin.sql*. The exact names of these files may be different on some operating systems. Check the Oracle installation and administration guides provided for your operating system for the exact names.

Here's an example of my *glogin.sql* file on my PC that displays the time and instance name in my SQL*PLUS prompt. The file also contains a few formatting commands to format SQL*PLUS output.

🖫 Glogin.sql

```
COLUMN file_name FORMAT a44
COLUMN tablespace_name FORMAT a20
COLUMN owner FORMAT a15
COLUMN segment_name FORMAT a20
set lines 132
set pages 100
set termout off
col dbname new_value prompt_dbname
select instance_name dbname from v$instance;
set sqlprompt "&&prompt_dbname> "
set termout on
set time on
```

Choosing a Database Block Size

Many database specifications can be changed after the database has been created. For releases prior to Oracle9i, one important exception is the database block size. Although Oracle9i allows you to specify different block sizes, choosing the default block size for an Oracle9i database is still critical.

Configuring the Oracle database to use bigger blocks often leads to an increase in performance since bigger blocks allow more data to be transferred per I/O call (the database block is the unit of I/O for the database engine). Larger blocks sizes also allow more key values to be stored in B-tree index blocks, which reduces the index's height and improves the performance of SQL statements that use the index structures.

Since you are storing more data per block, bigger blocks may increase the number of transactions that access data and index blocks concurrently. If you have a very high number of concurrent users, you may need to adjust the *initrans* and *maxtrans* parameters for data objects that have a higher than normal transactional concurrency.

A few quick thoughts on database block sizes:

- A block size of 2048 used to be the preferred database block size. This was before the era of high-speed disk drives and controllers. Now that more data can be transferred more quickly, 2048 has been replaced with 8192.

- A database block size of 8192 is currently the recommended block size for most database configurations.

- Use database block sizes of 16K and 32K for applications that have row sizes greater than 8K. If the application data has row sizes that are greater than 8K, using 16K or 32K block sizes allows more rows to be stored per block and decreases the I/O costs of accessing a single or multiple row(s).

- Use database block sizes of 16K and 32K for data warehouses and decision support systems. Decision support systems and data warehouses, by their nature, access large volumes of data to provide users with the information required to make business decisions. You will reduce disk I/O by storing more data in each block.

The Oracle Database Fundamentals I (1Z0-031) and the Oracle Database Performance Tuning (1Z0-033) certification tests will have a few questions on database blocks. Test candidates should know:

- The *db_block_size* parameter
- How to specify non standard block sizes in Oracle9i
- What tablespaces must use the default Oracle block size
- How to change the default Oracle block size
- The contents of an Oracle block
- What affect the PCTFREE and PCTUSED parameters have on data block free space
- The differences between PCTFREE/PCTUSED and automatic segment space management

- What row chaining and row migration are and the affect they have on database performance
- How to correctly size the default Oracle block size

Copying Databases Between Servers

Don't use the EXPORT/IMPORT utility to copy databases between servers running the same operating system. Execute the following steps to speed the transfer:

1. Execute the ALTER DATABASE BACKUP CONTROLFILE TO TRACE; statement on the source server.

2. Bring the database down and copy the trace file, parameter file, all datafiles, control files and redo logs to the new server.

3. Make the following changes to the trace file created in step 1:

4. If you are changing the database name, change the first line of the create statement to reflect the new name and change the REUSE keyword to SET.

5. Change NORESETLOGS to RESETLOGS.

6. Change directory names if they have changed on the new database server.

7. Delete all comments and lines that have a # in front of them (#s aren't comments in all Oracle tools).

8. Connect as INTERNAL and run the SQL statement contained in the trace file. It will start up the database in NOMOUNT stage and recreate the control files. The SQL statement's final step will be to MOUNT and then OPEN the database.

What happens if you can't take the database down? You'll have to execute a hot backup, which means your database will have to be in ARCHIVELOG mode. Here are the steps you will have to perform to copy an online database to a new server.

- Execute the hot backup, making sure all of the files are backed up. Note the time after the last tablespace is backed up.

- Execute ALTER SYSTEM SWITCH LOGFILE; to archive the last redo log that was active during the hot backup.

- Execute the ALTER DATABASE BACKUP CONTROLFILE TO TRACE; statement on the source server.

- Execute the ALTER DATABASE BACKUP CONTROLFILE TO *filename*; statement on the source server.

- Copy the datafile backups, both controlfile backups (backup to trace, backup to *filename*) and the archived redo logs that were generated during the hot backups. Make sure you match the directory structures that are on the source platform.

- Execute the RECOVER DATABASE UNTIL TIME XXXXX USING BACKUP CONTROLFILE; to recover the database on the new platform. Pick a time just after the hot backup was complete. If the file or directory names will be different on the target server, bring the database to MOUNT stage and issue the ALTER DATABASE RENAME FILE *oldfilename* TO *newfilename* command to point the control file to the new locations.

- If you need to change the database name, execute the following changes to the trace file created in step 1:
    - Change the first line of the create statement to reflect the new name and change the REUSE keyword to SET.
    - Change NORESETLOGS to RESETLOGS.
    - Change directory names if they have changed on the new database server.
    - Delete all comments and lines that have a # in front of them (#s aren't comments in all Oracle tools).
    - Connect as INTERNAL and run the SQL statement contained in the trace file. It will start up the database in NOMOUNT stage and recreate the control files. The SQL statement's final step will be to MOUNT and then OPEN the database.

Oracle Tablespaces

Students that are new to Oracle often become confused when instructors begin discussing Oracle's logical and physical storage structures. Every Oracle database is made up of data files that contain the database's data. The logical database structures (tables, indexes, etc.) define and format the data that is physically stored in the datafiles. The logical storage structure that ties the physical structures (files, blocks of data) to the logical structures (tables, indexes, etc.) is the tablespace. The DBA specifies the datafile name, size, and location during tablespace creation. The physical datafile(s) are created when the create tablespace statement is executed.

The DBA then assigns various logical objects to a specific tablespace during their creation.

Temporary Tablespaces

Sorting rows as efficiently as possible is one of the keys to high performance database applications. Oracle will automatically perform sorting operations on row data requested by CREATE INDEX, SQL ORDER BY, SQL GROUP BY statements and some join operations. For optimal performance, most sorts should occur in memory. Oracle8i allocates a private sort area (defined by the *sort_area_size* and *sort_area_retained_size* parameters) while Oracle9i also allows a shared sort area (*pga_aggregate_target* parameter) to be defined.

For many applications, sorting on disk cannot be avoided. Administrators are able to increase the performance of disk sorts by creating a tablespace that is optimized for sorting. Data sorted in a permanent tablespace requires many space allocation calls to allocate and deallocate temporary segments. If a sort tablespace is declared to be temporary, all processes requesting a sort operation share one sort segment in that tablespace. The first user process to sort creates the initial sort segment. All other sort operations share that sort segment by taking extents in the segment that was initially created.

Temporary tablespaces improve the performance of sorts that cannot be performed completely in memory. The performance benefits of bypassing the normal space allocation mechanism should not be taken lightly. The processing costs of each space allocation/deallocation execution can be roughly compared to the resources consumed by ten insert/update/delete statements.

You create a temporary tablespace to be temporary by using the TEMPORARY keyword of the CREATE TABLESPACE and ALTER TABLESPACE commands. It is important to note that temporary tablespaces cannot contain permanent objects (tables, indexes, rollback segments, etc.).

The Oracle Database Fundamentals I (1Z0-031) and the Oracle Database Performance Tuning (1Z0-033) certification tests will have a few questions on temporary tablespaces. Test candidates should have a firm understanding of:

- What the temporary tablespace is used for
- The differences between permanent and a temporary tablespace used for sorting
- How to create a default temporary tablespace in Oracle9i
- The impact default temporary tablespaces have on user administration

Where the user sorts if a default temporary tablespace is not specified

Create Tablespace Temporary vs. Create Temporary Tablespace

The Oracle SQL reference manual provides two different statements to create a temporary tablespace:

- CREATE TABLESPACE temp DATAFILE 'd:\oradata\orcl\tempdata.dbf.' The statement above creates a tablespace that, although described as "temporary" in *dba_tablespaces*, has one or more permanent datafiles associated with it. The tablespace is designed to hold sort data and manages segments and extents differently (see above) than its permanent tablespace counterparts.

- CREATE TEMPORARY TABLESPACE temp TEMPFILE 'd:\oradata\tempdata.dbf.' This statement creates a true temporary tablespace. This eliminates the need to back up the temporary tablespace, which results in faster backups and a reduction in disk space. Information describing true temporary tablespaces is found in the *v$tempfile* and *dba_temp_file* views. No information is stored in the *dba_data_files* and *v$datafile* views, which describe permanent datafiles.

The database will start even if this file is missing. The only way the administrator will know that the file is gone is when the first sort tries to overflow to disk. A very explicit error message will be generated stating that the sort could not complete due to a missing or invalid sort file. The administrator will be forced to drop and recreate the temporary tablespace before sorting to disk can take place.

Partitioning

Data partitioning is an absolute requirement for the administration and management of large database tables and indexes. In Oracle, a partitioned table is divided into components called tablespace partitions (see Figure 1). All table partitions have the same logical attributes (columns, datatypes, and integrity constraints). Oracle allows administrators to store each partition in a separate tablespace. Separate tablespaces allow each partition to have different physical storage characteristics (PCTFREE, PCTUSED, PCTINCREASE etc.).

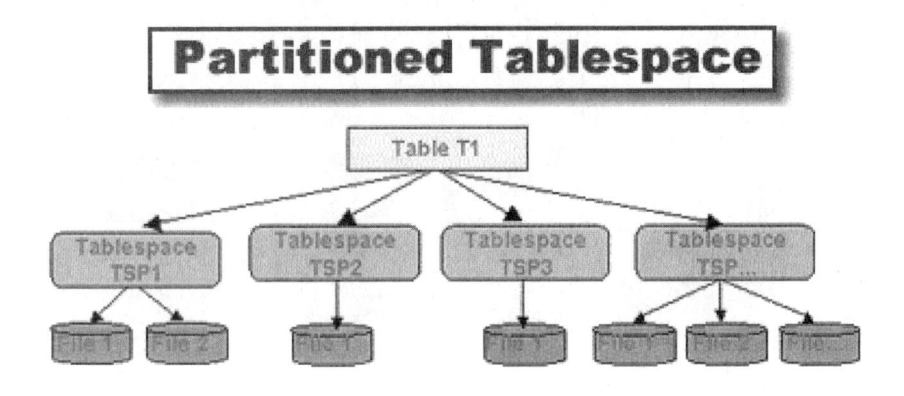

Figure 1: *Partitioned tablespace.*

Partitioning of data into separate tablespaces provides the following advantages:

- Increases availability - Data corruption is less likely to occur across multiple tablespaces. If data does become corrupted in a single, partitioned tablespace, all other partitions are still available for queries and DML. In addition, you can perform certain administrative operations against a single tablespace partition. Once again, all other tablespace partitions remain unaffected and are available for access.

- Easier administration - Administrative operations (import/export, analyze, backup/recovery and load) can be performed on individual partitions. Remaining partitioned tablespaces continue to be available for access.

- Partitioning allows applications to take advantage of "rolling window" data operations (refer to figure 2). Rolling windows allow administrators to roll off (and un-plug data using Oracle's transportable tablespace feature) that are no longer needed. For example, a DBA may roll off the data in the tablespace containing last April's data as they add this year's data for April. If the data is ever needed again, administrators are able to pull the data from tape and plug the data back into the database using the transportable tablespace.

Figure 2: *Rolling windows data operations.*

- Increases performance - Partitioning allows you to distribute data and balance the I/O load across several devices. The Oracle optimizer is partition aware and will create query plans that access only those partitions and subpartitions needed to satisfy the query's request (partition pruning). Partition pruning is critical in providing quick access to data that is logically grouped together (i.e. date, customer id, etc.).

Partition pruning (see Figure 3) allows administrators to create large data stores and still provide fast access to the data. There is no difference in query performance between a 20 GIG database and a 200 GIG database if the optimizer prunes the data to create access paths to only those partitions required to solve the query. Partitioned tablespaces also increase the performance of bulk data loads. Oracle's SQL*Loader supports concurrent loading of individual partitions and entire partitioned tables.

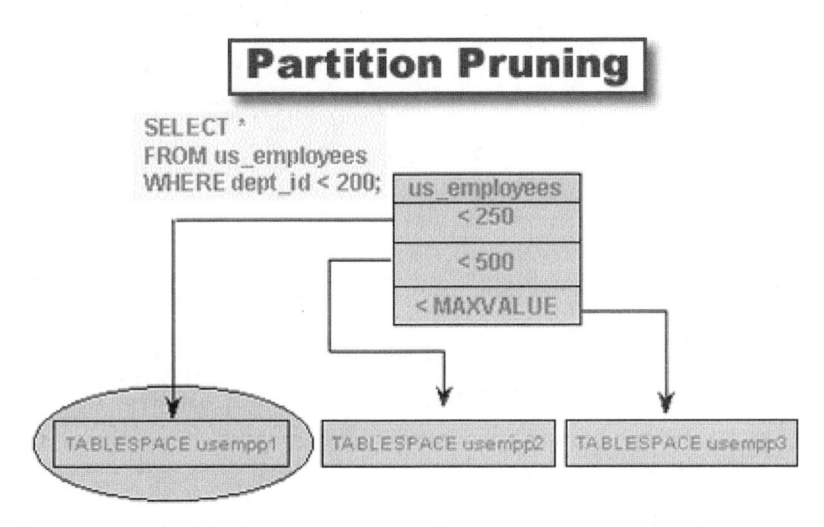

Figure 3: *Partition pruning.*

Oracle 8 - Range Partitioning

Oracle8 introduced the first partitioning technique called range partitioning. To create a range partitioned table in Oracle, you code a partitioning clause for the table that includes a key-based specification that is used to map rows to specific partitions and a partition description that describes each partition:

```
CREATE TABLE sales_account_history_data
(acct_no NUMBER (5),
person VARCHAR2 (30),
week_no NUMBER (2))
PARTITION BY RANGE (week_no)
     (PARTITION p1 VALUES LESS THAN (4) TABLESPACE TSP1,
      PARTITION p2 VALUES LESS THAN (8) TABLESPACE TSP2,
      ...
      PARTITION px VALUES LESS THAN(53) TABLESPACE TSPx);
```

Rows are placed in the different partitions based on the table's partitioning key. A partitioning key is a column or set of columns that is associated with a specific tablespace. The example above shows a table that is partitioned by a range of values based on a number.

With range partitioning, the best partition keys are dates, primary keys or foreign key columns. To prevent the overhead associated with migrating rows among partitions, application programs should not update partitioning key columns. To change a value in one of these columns, the application program should delete the row and then reinsert it with the new values. To define a partition, an upper boundary of partitioning key values is hard-coded into the table's definition. These upper boundaries should distribute the data (more or less) evenly among the different partitions.

Index Partitioning

Oracle also allows you to create range-partitioned indexes. Oracle uses the same range-partitioning algorithm as it does for tables. Like partitioned tables, Oracle maps rows to specific index partitions based on the index's partitioning key. The partitioning key of an index must include one or more of the columns that define the index. This allows administrators to create an index that contains multiple columns but partitions the index on a subset of those columns. An index partition is defined exactly like its partitioned table counterpart; an upper boundary of partitioning key values is hard-coded into each tablespace specification.

Equi-Partitioned Objects

An index and table that has the same number of partitions are said to be equi-partitioned. Multiple tables and multiple indexes can be equi-partitioned if they meet Oracle's equi-partition specifications. Please refer to the Oracle Server Concepts manual for a more complete listing of equi-partitioning specifications.

Equi-partitioned objects improve query performance by reducing the number of rows being sorted and joined. The Oracle optimizer is also partition aware. If the optimizer determines that a single index/table partition combination will satisfy a query, it will create an execution plan that accesses the single index and table partition.

Local Indexes

You can ensure that a table and its associated index are equi-partitioned by specifying the *local* parameter during index creation. All keys in a local index partition point to rows stored in a single table partition. When creating an index using the *local* parameter, range specifications and a maximum value do not need to be specified. Oracle automatically partitions the local index on the same partitioning key columns as the table it references, creates the same number of partitions and gives each index partition the same partitioning key boundaries.

Global Indexes

Unlike their local index counterparts, index keys in a global index may point to rows in more than one table partition (see Figure 4). To create a global index, you specify the GLOBAL parameter (default) during index creation. Global indexes can be equi-partitioned with their tables that they reference, but Oracle will not take advantage of equi-partitioning when generating query plans or executing maintenance operations. The entire index will be affected. To take advantage of Oracle's equi-partitioned performance improvements, the index must be created as *local*.

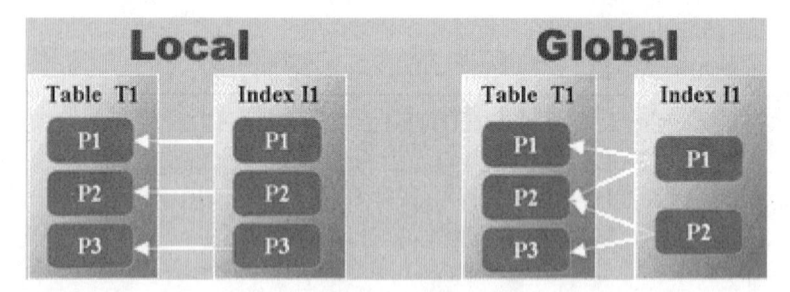

Figure 4: *Index keys in a global index.*

Oracle8i – Hash and Range/Hash Composite Partitioning

Oracle8i enhanced the Oracle database's partitioning feature by providing two new partitioning techniques, hash and range/hash composite.

Hash Partitioning

Hash partitioning allows data to be evenly striped across devices. Hash partitioning uses a hashing algorithm on the partitioning columns to determine row placement in the tablespaces. The more unique the key values are, the more efficient the hashing algorithm will be. In general, the hash-partitioning key should be unique or near unique.

Hash partitioning attempts to evenly divide data among all available partitions. There is no way for the administrator to logically group data together in a partition. As a result, hash partitioning prohibits "partition pruning" from occurring. Hash partitioning also prevents "rolling window" operations from occurring. Rolling windows allow administrators to roll off data that is no longer needed.

Combining Range and Hash Partitioning – Range/Hash Composite Partitioning

Range/hash composite partitioning combines the best of both approaches. A range of values first partitions data then each partition is sub-partitioned into several hash partitions. This provides administrators with the ability to provide customized partitioning per application. The user specifies ranges of values for the primary partitions of the table or index then specifies a number of hash subpartitions.

Oracle9i – List and Range/List Composite Partitioning

Oracle9i continues to add partitioning functionality to the Oracle database by providing two new partitioning algorithms, list and range/list composite.

List Partitioning

List partitioning allows the administrator to map a row to a specific tablespace based on the partitioning key value. The partition is defined by specifying a hard-coded list of individual partition key values. In Oracle9i Release 1, there was no overflow area to hold rows that had keys that were not identified in the list specifications. If an application program attempted to insert a row that had a partitioning key value that did not match any of the specifications, the row was not inserted and an Oracle error code was returned.

Oracle9i Release 2 solves this problem by allowing administrators to specify a default partition. Key values that do not match the list partition specifications are placed in the overflow tablespace. A new DEFAULT attribute has been added to the list partition specification. The example below shows the DEFAULT attribute being specified during partitioned table creation:

```
CREATE TABLE sales
(salesid NUMBER(9999), transdate DATE, state VARCHAR2(30)…..)
PARTITION BY LIST (state)
(PARTITION region_north VALUES ('New York', 'Maine')
    PARTITION region_south VALUES ('Florida', 'Georgia')
……….
PARTITION region_ovflw VALUES (DEFAULT));
```

Range/List Composite Partitioning

Oracle's latest release offers a hybrid solution for list partitioning that is a combination of the range and list partitioning techniques. The table is first partitioned by range and then subpartitioned using the list partitioning technique. Unlike composite range-hash partitioning, each subpartition contains a logical division of the data that is specified by the DBA (as opposed to the range-hash technique where the subpartitions are selected by the hashing algorithm itself).

For example, the primary partition could be based on a date range to allow rolling window operations to occur and the second level could be based on a logical grouping (a list of states (i.e. Pennsylvania, New York, Ohio, etc.) is an good example of a logical grouping). The data would be divided according to the date range and divided again according to the state's name. The example below shows a table using the range-list composite partitioning technique:

```
CREATE TABLE sales
(salesid NUMBER(9999), transdate DATE, state VARCHAR2(30)…..)
PARTITION BY RANGE (transdate)
SUBPARTITION BY LIST (state)
SUBPARTITION TEMPLATE
(PARTITION region_north VALUES ('New York', 'Maine')
     PARTITION region_south VALUES ('Florida', 'Georgia'))

     (PARTITION 2002_quarter1 values less than
         (TO_DATE ('01-APR-2002', 'DD-MON-YYYY')),
      PARTITION 2002_quarter2 values less than……..
```

The CREATE TABLE partitioned tablespace above uses the SUBPARTITION TEMPLATE clause to define the subpartitions. If all subpartitions have the same definition, administrators are able to code the subpartition specification once and Oracle will apply the template specification to each main partition that does not override the template with its own subpartition specification. If the template were not used, the subpartition clause would have to be specified after each main partition specification.

Which Partitioning Technique Do I Choose?

Choose range partitioning when the partitioning keys have distinct ranges that can be easily defined and do not vary dramatically. The problem with range partitioning is trying to determine what the range specifications are. The DBA should select a range of values that evenly divides the data among the individual tablespace partitions. Dates are excellent candidates for range partitioning keys because they allow the previously discussed rolling window operations to occur. If range partitioning will result in partitions that vary dramatically in size because of unequal key distribution, the DBA should consider other partitioning techniques.

If the DBA wants to use partitioning for performance and manageability but there are no columns that have distinct key ranges, the hash partitioning technique provides an excellent alternative. Since the rows are mapped based on a hashing algorithm, the higher the cardinality (the number of different values) the partitioning key contains, the more evenly the data will be divided among the different partitions. Many DBAs create an artificial series of numbers that are used as input to the hashing algorithm. These unique values ensure that the hashing algorithm evenly divides the rows among the tablespace partitions.

If you need specific control over the mapping of rows to tablespace partitions, use the list partitioning technique. List partitioning allows the DBA to logically group the data among the different partitions. Sales region would be an excellent example of a column that would lend itself to the list partitioning technique. The DBA would be able to divide the data among the partitions based on the company's different sales regions.

Range/hash composite partitioning provides the manageability and availability benefits of range partitioning with the data distribution advantages of hash partitioning. Data skew is unlikely, because the user can always add or drop subpartitions within a partition to maintain even distribution of each container. Rolling windows of historical data are easily maintained by adding or dropping primary partitions with no effect on subpartitions in other primary partitions.

The range-list composite partitioning method provides for partitioning based on a two-level hierarchy. For example, the primary partition could be based on a date range to allow rolling window operation to occur and the second level could be based on a logical grouping (a list of state codes (i.e. PA, NY, OH, etc.) is an good example of a logical grouping). The data would be divided according to the date range and divided again according to the state's abbreviation.

The Oracle Database Performance Tuning (1Z0-033) certification test will contain a few questions on tablespace partitioning. Test candidates should understand:

- The basic partitioning algorithms (range, list, hash, composite)
- How to specify partitioning during table creation
- When to use a specific partitioning algorithm

Oracle9i Tablespace Changes

Oracle9*i* provides the database administrator with a variety (read that bewildering array) of new tablespace parameters and block sizes. Administrators are now able to create Oracle managed tablespaces, user managed tablespaces, locally managed tablespaces, dictionary managed tablespaces, specify AUTOALLOCATE, UNIFORM, PERMANENT, UNDO as well as select block sizes of 2K, 4K, 8K, 16K, or 32K.

The tablespace definition below combines a few of the aforementioned options:

```
CREATE TABLESPACE oracle_local_auto DATAFILE SIZE 5M BLOCKSIZE
2K;
```

Many of the parameters were not specified intentionally to highlight some of the default specifications for Oracle9i tablespaces. Although some of the parameters we will review were introduced in earlier releases, it is important to discuss them to obtain a clear understanding of tablespace administration in Oracle9i. Let's continue our discussion by taking a closer look at the tablespace's definition:

- Because a datafile specification was not provided, the tablespace is Oracle managed. The datafile clause is only optional if the DB_CREATE_FILE_DEST initialization parameter is set. The parameter specifies an operating system directory that is the default storage location for Oracle managed datafiles. The operating system directory must already exist and must have the proper security permissions to allow Oracle to create files in it. If a datafile specification and SIZE parameter are not specified, a 100-megabyte file is created by default. During tablespace creation, the database server selects a file name for the Oracle managed file and creates the file in the directory specified in the *db_create_file_dest* initialization parameter. When the tablespace is dropped, Oracle automatically removes the Oracle managed files associated with the dropped tablespace. By default, an Oracle managed datafile is autoextensible with an unlimited maximum size.

- The tablespace will be locally managed because we did not specify EXTENT MANAGEMENT DICTIONARY during creation. Oracle has changed the default from dictionary managed in Oracle8i to locally managed in Oracle9i. Locally managed tablespaces track all extent information in the tablespace itself, using bitmaps. Tracking extents in bitmaps improves speed and concurrency of space operations.

  Administrators are able to override Oracle managed extents by specifying EXTENT MANAGEMENT DICTIONARY in the tablespace definition. Dictionary managed tablespaces rely on data dictionary tables to track space utilization within the tablespace. The SYSTEM tablespace is always dictionary managed.

- The tablespace will use the default free space management setting of SEGMENT SPACE MANAGEMENT MANUAL. As a result, Oracle will use freelists to manage free space within segments in the tablespace. Free lists are lists of data blocks that have space available for inserting rows.

Administrators have the option of overriding the default specification of SEGMENT SPACE MANAGEMENT MANAUAL with SEGMENT SPACE MANAGEMENT AUTO. SEGMENT SPACE MANAGEMENT AUTO tells Oracle to use bitmaps to manage free space within a segment. The bitmap structure stores information that describes the amount of space in the blocks that are available for row inserts. As free space within each block grows and shrinks, its new state is reflected in the bitmap. Bitmaps allow Oracle to manage free space more automatically. As a result, tracking free space within segments using bitmaps provides a simpler and more efficient method of free space management. Only permanent, locally managed tablespaces can specify automatic segment space management.

- The extent management will be AUTOALLOCATE (extent sizes defined and managed by Oracle) because a default storage clause is not be specified. If the default storage clause is not specified, or if it is specified with PCTINCREASE not equal to 0 and/or INITIAL not equal to NEXT, then Oracle creates a locally managed tablespace with extents managed automatically (AUTOALLOCATE).

  Administrators are also able to specify that the tablespace is managed with uniform extents of a specific size by specifying UNIFORM SIZE in the tablespace's definition or by specifying INITIAL = NEXT and PCTINCREASE = 0. This specification tells Oracle to create a uniform locally managed tablespace with uniform extent size = INITIAL.

- The tablespace datafile will have a 2K blocksize. Oracle9i allows administrators to specify a nonstandard block size for tablespaces. In order for the tablespace specification to override the standard database blocksize specified during database creation, the *db_cache_size* and *db_nk_cache_size* (where n*k* matches the tablespace block size) must be set in the initialization parameter file. Oracle9i allows administrators to choose from 2K, 4K, 8K, 16K and 32K blocksizes.

- Finally, it will be autoextensible (the file will be able to automatically grow in size) because autoextensible is the default for an Oracle managed file.

Let's take a look at our tablespace definition again. This time we will provide all of the specifications for some of the features we have just discussed:

```
CREATE TABLESPACE oracle_local_auto DATAFILE SIZE 5M BLOCKSIZE
2K AUTOEXTEND ON EXTENT MANAGEMENT LOCAL SEGMENT SPACE
MANAGEMENT MANUAL;
```

Oracle9i's new tablespace definitions allow administrators to tailor their environments to meet application requirements. We'll end our discussion on Oracle9i tablespaces with a few quick recommendations:

- Oracle managed – In addition to the benefits of not needing to create filenames and define specific storage requirements, managed files provide the additional advantage of being deleted from the operating system when the DROP TABLESPACE statement is executed. But these benefits do not outweigh the disadvantage of losing the flexibility of specifying different mountpoints or drives manually. Most administrators will prefer to have the flexibility of placing files on different drives or mountpoints and to not be forced into using one directory specification (whether that directory is striped or not).

- Multiple block sizes — Multiple blocksize specifications allow administrators to tailor physical storage specifications to a data object's size and usage to maximize I/O performance. In addition, it also allows administrators to easily use the transportable tablespace feature to transfer tablespaces between databases having different default blocksizes (i.e. moving data from an OLTP application to a data warehouse).

- Locally managed — Oracle is highly recommending that locally managed tablespaces be used for all tablespaces. Because extent management is tracked internally, the need to coalesce tablespaces is no longer required. In addition, allocating or releasing space in a locally managed tablespace avoids recursive space management operations (updates to data dictionary tables that track space utilization). Oracle also states that data objects with high numbers of extents have less of a performance impact on locally managed tablespaces than they do on their dictionary managed counterparts.

The Oracle Database Fundamentals I (1Z0-031) and the Oracle Database Performance Tuning (1Z0-033) certification tests will have numerous questions on Oracle tablespaces. Test candidates should have a thorough understanding of Oracle tablespaces and datafiles. This knowledge should include:

- CREATE tablespace syntax
- Locally managed vs. dictionary managed tablespaces
- Datafile fragmentation

- Extent allocation in tablespaces (know how autoallocate and uniform size allocate extents)
- High-water marks
- Temporary tablespaces
- Permanent tablespaces
- Tablespace quotas
- What happens when a tablespace is set offline

Locally Managed System Tablespaces

Locally managed tablespaces allow the Oracle system to automatically manage an object's extents. Locally managed tablespaces track object information in bitmap structures stored in the tablespace itself. Oracle states that locally managed tablespaces provide increases in the concurrency and speed of space operations and generally have a positive impact on application performance.

In Oracle9i Release 2, administrators are now able to create a locally managed SYSTEM tablespace. The EXTENT MANAGEMENT LOCAL clause can be used to create a locally managed SYSTEM tablespace during database creation or administrators can use the stored procedure *dbms_space_admin.tablespace_migrate_to_local* to migrate existing dictionary managed tablespaces to locally managed. Once you create or migrate to a locally managed SYSTEM tablespace, you are unable to create any dictionary-managed tablespaces in the database.

Care must be taken when using the aforementioned package to migrate SYSTEM tablespaces from dictionary managed to locally managed. It is a requirement that all tablespaces (except those containing UNDO segments) be in READ ONLY mode for the migration process to successfully execute. If Oracle finds any tablespaces in READ WRITE mode, the error message states that the tablespaces must be placed in READ ONLY mode.

The problem is that if the administrator places any dictionary-managed tablespaces in READ ONLY mode, they will be unable to place them in READ WRITE mode after the SYSTEM tablespace is converted to locally managed. Administrators desiring to migrate their SYSTEM tablespaces to locally managed must migrate all READ WRITE dictionary managed tablespaces to locally managed tablespaces BEFORE MIGRATING THE SYSTEM TABLESPACE.

Rollback Segments

A transaction uses a rollback segment to record before images of data it intends to change. If the transaction fails before committing, Oracle uses the before images to rollback or undo the uncommitted data changes. Oracle also uses rollback segments for statement-level read consistency. Read consistency ensures that all data returned by a query comes from the same point-in-time (query start time). Lastly, rollback segments provide before images of data to help the instance roll back failed transactions during instance recovery.

When is the System Rollback Segment Used?

When you create a database, Oracle creates a rollback segment called system in the system tablespace. The system rollback segment is only used for transactions that occur inside the system tablespace. The system rollback segment's main purpose is to handle the rollback generated for DDL statements. DDL statements cause updates to be applied to the data dictionary tables in the system tablespace. It is possible for the system rollback segment to be used for non-data dictionary tables, but only if those tables are created inside the system tablespace (which is very bad development practice).

Rollback Segments and Transaction Processing Workloads

In releases prior to Oracle9i, sizing rollback segments is more of an art than a science. The key to good rollback segment performance is monitoring the statistics associated with rollback segment waits, sizing and activity. The queries below provide information that can be used to tune rollback segments:

```
SELECT CLASS, COUNT FROM V$WAITSTAT WHERE CLASS = '%undo%.'
```

Any non-zero value in the count column indicates rollback segment contention. Consider creating more rollback segments and begin analyzing rollback segment sizing specifications.

```
SELECT rn.Name "Rollback Segment", rs.RSSize/1024 "Size (KB)",
rs.Gets "Gets", rs.waits "Waits", (rs.Waits/rs.Gets)*100 "%
Waits", rs.Shrinks "# Shrinks", rs.Extends "# Extends" FROM
sys.v_$RollName rn, sys.v_$RollStat rs WHERE rn.usn = rs.usn.
```

Besides the obvious columns (waits, %waits) take a look at the number of shrinks and extends that are occurring. High numbers indicate that the specifications that

Rollback Segments

control the size of the rollback segment (INITIAL, NEXT, MINEXTENTS, OPTIMAL) may need to be increased.

```
SELECT segment_name, bytes, extents FROM dba_segments WHERE
segment_type = 'ROLLBACK.'
```

The simplest query of the three can also be the most helpful. The query should be run when database activity is high. Active rollback segments don't have a chance to shrink back to their optimal settings. The query will help the DBA to determine if the rollback segments' sizing specifications (INITIAL, NEXT, MINEXTENTS, OPTIMAL) are set sufficiently large enough. If the report shows that the rollback segments are allocating high numbers of extents, further sizing analysis is warranted.

Batch and On-line Processing

Applications that consist of batch jobs that perform heavy DML processing (UPDATE, INSERT, DELETE) and on-line transactions that perform minimal updates complicate the rollback segment sizing process. The ultimate solution is to have:

- The on-line transactions use smaller rollback segments. Smaller rollback segments have a greater chance to be cached in memory and are more quickly allocated than their larger counterparts.

- The heavy DML processing batch transactions use the larger rollback segments. Larger rollback segment extents means less extents required to hold before images and an increase in performance (due to the overhead of extent allocation).

The SET TRANSACTION USE ROLLBACK SEGMENT xxxx command can be used to control the placement of these large (or small) transactions. The SET TRANSACTION statement allows the developer to "point" their transaction to a particular rollback segment.

If the bulk of the heavy DML processing is done during off-hours, the DBA is able to "switch" rollback segments on and off by running batch scripts that execute the ALTER ROLLBACK SEGMENT xxxx (OFFLINE/ONLINE) command. Before the nightly batch run begins, a script can be automatically executed to bring the large rollback segments on-line and the small rollback segments off-line. The last step of the nightly batch run performs the reverse. The smaller rollback segments are brought on-line while their larger counterparts are turned off.

Rollback Segments and Users – Who's Using What?

The output from the query below will tell you what rollback segment a user is using. The output provides the rollback segment name, Oracle account and operating system account. This is a good statement to use when an active transaction is preventing a rollback segment from being taken offline or shrinking back to its optimal size.

```
select osuser o, username u, segment_name s,
substr(sa.sql_text,1,200) txt
from v$session s, v$transaction t, dba_rollback_segs r,
v$sqlarea sa
where s.taddr=t.addr and t.xidusn=r.segment_id(+) and
s.sql_address=sa.address(+)
```

The statement provides the OS user account, Oracle account, the rollback (or undo) segment name and the statement that is currently executing.

Oracle9i - Database Managed Undo Segments

You don't have to be an Oracle expert to know that rollback segments can be "somewhat troublesome." Out of space conditions, contention, poor performance and the perennial favorite "snap shot too old" errors have been plaguing Oracle database administrators for over a decade. Oracle finally decided that the database could probably do a better job of managing before images of data than we could.

In Oracle9i, administrators have their choice of continuing to manage rollback segments on their own (manual undo management) or configuring the database to manage its own before image data (automatic undo management). Oracle refers to system managed before image segments as undo segments.

Administrators must create a tablespace to hold undo segments by using the new UNDO keyword in the tablespace create statement:

```
CREATE UNDO TABLESPACE undots1
    DATAFILE 'undotbs_1a.f'
    SIZE 10M AUTOEXTEND ON;
```

The following initialization parameters are used to activate automatic undo management:

- *undo_management* – AUTO configures the database is to use automatic undo segments. MANUAL configures the database to use rollback segments.

- *undo_tablespace* – Specifies the tablespaces that are to be used to hold the undo segments. The tablespace must be created using the UNDO keyword. If no tablespace is defined, Oracle will select the first available undo tablespace. If no undo tablespaces are present in the database, Oracle will use the system rollback segment during startup. This value can be set dynamically by using the ALTER SYSTEM statement.

- *undo_retention* – specifies the amount of time that Oracle attempts to keep undo data available. This parameter becomes important when the Oracle9i flashback query option is used.

You cannot create database objects in undo tablespaces. It is reserved for system-managed undo data. The view *dba_undo_extents* can be accessed to retrieve information relating to system managed undo data. For those of us familiar with *v$rollstat*, it is still available and the information reflects the behavior of the undo segments in the undo tablespace.

We found automatic undo management to be pretty reliable during our initial beta testing of Oracle9i. The key to success is to allocate sufficient disk storage to the undo tablespace and to set AUTOEXTEND on to allow

Oracle9i - Database Managed Undo Segments   **121**

the tablespace datafiles to grow automatically. During our beta testing, numerous heavy batch update jobs were simultaneously run to simulate heavy work loads. We found that the system managed undo segments worked as advertised. During performance comparisons, we did find that system managed undo segments did seem to add some extra processing time to the batch loads. We found that the rollback segment tablespace used in our comparison testing auto extended sooner than its system managed undo tablespace counterpart. One possible explanation is that the overhead can be attributed to the system managed undo segments performing additional actions to squeeze more undo data in the tablespace before giving up and auto expanding the undo tablespace datafile.

All of the Oracle certification tests will have numerous questions on undo segments. Test candidates should have a strong knowledge of undo segments including:

- What rollback segments are used for
    - Transaction rollback
    - Transaction recovery
    - Read consistency
- The parameters used to activate automatic undo management
    - *undo_management*
    - *undo_tablespace*
    - *undo_retention*
- The differences between automatic undo management and manual undo management

- What "snapshot too old" error messages and how to avoid them

- Although the test covers Oracle9i, candidates should also have a firm understanding of manual undo (rollback) segments

- You must know the contents of *v$undostat* and how it is used to size undo segment tablespaces

Redo Logs (roll forward recovery)

On-line and archived redo logs are the base components of the Oracle instance and roll-forward recovery processes. Redo logs must also be sized correctly to obtain optimal performance.

Checkpoint Not Complete

Checkpoints ensure that all modified data buffers are written to the database files. One (out of several) reasons Oracle can fire a checkpoint is when it switches from one log group to another. When Oracle fills a log group, a checkpoint is fired and Oracle then begins writing to the next log group. This continues in a circular fashion; when all log groups are filled Oracle reuses the first group. The process by which DBWR writes modified data buffers to disk in Oracle is not synchronized with the COMMIT of the corresponding transactions. The checkpoint ensures that all the modified data buffers in the cache that are covered by the current log are written to the corresponding data files.

A common rule of thumb is to adjust the redo log's size so that Oracle performs a log switch every 15 to 30 minutes. Log switches that occur more frequently may have a negative impact on performance. Log switches that occur several times a minute have a definite impact on database performance. Checking messages in the alert log is an easy way to determine how fast Oracle is filling and switching logs. If the following messages are found, you can be sure that performance is being affected:

```
Thread 1 advanced to log sequence 248
Current log# 2 seq# 248 mem# 0:
/orant/oradata/logs/redolog2a.log
Thread 1 cannot allocate new log, sequence 249
Checkpoint not complete
```

The "checkpoint not complete" messages are generated because the logs are switching so fast that the checkpoint associated with the log switch isn't complete. During that time, Oracle's LGWR process has filled up the other redo log groups and is now waiting for the first checkpoint to successfully execute. Oracle will stop processing until the checkpoint completes successfully.

Performance can be dramatically improved by increasing the log sizes so that logs switch at the recommended interval of 15 to 30 minutes. Identify the current size of the redo log members from *v$log*, record the number of log switches per hour and increase the size of the log to allow Oracle to switch at the recommended rate of one switch per 15 to 30 minutes. For example, if the database log size is 1 megabyte and you are switching logs every 1 minute, you will need to increase the log size to 30 megabytes in size to allow it to switch every 30 minutes.

The problem is that many applications have workloads that vary dramatically throughout each 24-hour time-period. In addition, application-processing workloads may vary according to the days of the calendar month. Month-end and mid-month processing may increase the number of changes occurring in the database. This higher level of activity may cause the redo logs to be filled much more quickly than during off-peak times. The DBA must make sure that the on-line redo logs don't switch too often during periods of high activity and switch often enough during times of low processing workloads.

The *log_checkpoint_timeout*, *log_checkpoint_interval* and *fast_smart_mttr_target* parameters come to the rescue. These parameters can be set to decrease the time of instance recoveries.

It is important to note that these parameters will not reduce the amount of data lost in certain database recovery scenarios. If a lost or damaged archived or online redo log is required as input to a database recovery, the amount of data lost will be directly proportional to the amount of time that the lost redo log was active. Since we now know that the size of the archived redo logs determine how long the log will be active, the larger the log the more data loss there will be!

Resizing Redo Logs

Now that we understand how to determine what sizes our redo logs should be, let's continue our discussion with some information on how to resize them. Before we begin resizing our redo logs, we need to review Oracle recommendations on redo log groups and members.

The administrator's guide states that each database should have at least three groups of redo logs with each group having at least two members each. In addition, Oracle recommends that all redo log group members be the same size.

If your redo log sizes are too small (or too large), they can be easily resized while the database is up and running. The steps to resize the redo logs are as follows:

- Determine how quickly the logs are switching by checking the database's alert log or the v$log_history view.

- Create a dummy redo log group containing one member. The size of the redo log group member should be large enough to give you enough time to complete the alterations below. 15 to 30 minutes should be enough time.

- Use the ALTER SYSTEM SWITCH LOGFILE statement to make the dummy the active log group. Use the view v$log to determine which group is active. Keep switching and checking until the dummy group becomes active.

- Drop the first redo log group (ALTER DATABASE DROP LOGFILE....) and then recreate the redo log group (ALTER DATABASE ADD LOGFILE....). If you try to drop a group that has become active for whatever reason, rest assured that Oracle is smarter than you are in this case and will prohibit you from doing so.

- Repeat the previous step until all of the permanent redo log groups have been resized.

- Drop the dummy log group by executing the ALTER DATABASE DROP LOGFILE… statement.

All of the Oracle certification tests will have numerous questions on redo logs. Test candidates should have a strong knowledge of redo and archived redo logs including:

- How the Oracle environment uses redo logs
- Redo log impact on database recovery and database performance
- How to administer redo logs
    - Creating
    - Adding members and groups
    - Dropping members and groups
    - Resizing redo logs
    - Clearing corrupt or missing archived redo logs
- Redo log archiving
    - The parameters used to activate and configure the archiving process
    - The impact archiving has on database recoveries
- Know what information is displayed when using the "ARCHIVE LOG LIST" command.

Oracle Tables and Indexes

In the next few sections, we will be discussing Oracle tables and indexes. Please note that this book is not intended to be a replacement for the Oracle reference manuals. Think of it as a collection of hints, tips, tricks and information the author thought may be beneficial. Once again, I'll include some performance information just to keep it lively.

Space Utilization for Parallel Table Creates

You must adjust the *initial* extent parameter for a table when using the parallel clause of the CREATE TABLE as SELECT * FROM statement. All parallel processes will allocate an extent defined by the table's *initial* extent parameter. Here's an example:

```
CREATE TABLE test2 AS SELECT * FROM test1 STORAGE (INITIAL 2047M
NEXT 500M... PARALLEL 4;
```

The above statement would create a table that has 4 extents with each extent being 2047M in size.

Index-only Tables

Oracle8 allowed you to define an index-only table (see Figure 6) that keeps data sorted on the primary key. Oracle stores the table rows in a B-tree index built on the primary key. The B-tree index contains both the key value and the key value's corresponding row data.

Image 6: *Index-only tables.*

Index-only tables increase the performance of SQL statements by providing faster access to table data for queries that use the key value for exact value searches. Index-only tables also increase performance by eliminating the index to table I/O associated with conventional B-Tree index structures.

The first implementation of index-only tables contained many restrictions on their implementation and usage. One example is that secondary indexes were not allowed to be built on index-only tables in Oracle8. Oracle removed restrictions and enhanced index-only functionality with each subsequent release. It is important that the DBA check the Oracle administrator's guide for their release to determine how to correctly administer index-only tables.

Conventional B-tree index entries are quite small since they consist of a key value and ROWID. Index-only tables index entries can become quite large since they consist of a key value and the key value's corresponding row data. The B-tree index leaf nodes (bottom layer of the index) of an index-only table may end up storing a single row that effectively destroys the B-tree index's dense clustering property. Oracle8 uses a Row Overflow Area to overcome the problem of large B-tree index entries. You are able to define an overflow tablespace and a threshold value (% of block size) during index-only table creation. The following DDL creates an index-only table:

```
CREATE TABLE store_table
(store_id VARCHAR2 (10) CONSTRAINT pk_store_table PRIMARY KEY,
store_address VARCHAR2 (200),
store_manager VARCHAR2 (50))
ORGANIZATION INDEX TABLESPACE store_table_tspace
PCTTHRESHOLD 20
OVERFLOW TABLESPACE store_table _ovflw;
```

The previous DDL is interpreted as follows:

- The primary key of the store_table is the store_id column. A primary key must be specified for index-only tables.

- The ORGANIZATION INDEX specification indicates that the store_table is an index-only table. The row data resides in an index defined on the store_id column that is the store_table's primary key.

- The OVERFLOW TABLESPACE specification indicates that rows that exceed 20% of the table's blocksize will be placed in the store_table_ovflw tablespace.

Single Table Hash Clusters

Hashing is another way of storing table data to improve the performance of data retrieval. The administrator first creates the hash cluster storage object and then creates the tables specifying the cluster as the storage mechanism. Oracle physically stores the rows of a table in a hash cluster and retrieves them according to the results of a hash function (much like the IMS hierarchical database).

The hash function uses a key value to calculate an address, which corresponds to a specific data block in the cluster. A cluster key column value is specified during the creation of the cluster. The key values for a hash cluster can be loosely compared to index key values as they can consist of a single key column or composite key column (multiple table columns make up the key).

To insert or retrieve a row from the hash cluster, Oracle uses the hash function to calculate the address of the data block the row is stored in. To find a row by using an index, Oracle must traverse the index to find the key value/ROWID combination and then incur additional I/O to read the row from the table. Because the hash function calculates the block address of the requested row, no index searches are required.
Oracle allows users to store multiple tables in a hash cluster. Table rows that have matching cluster key values are stored in the same data block. As a result, applications that retrieve rows from clustered tables based on the tables' cluster key values reduce I/O consumption by being able to find rows from both tables in the same data block.

The Oracle9i Performance and Tuning Guide states, " In an ordinary hash cluster, Oracle scans all the rows for a given table in the block, even if there is only one row with the matching key. Oracle8i introduced single-table

Single Table Hash Clusters **131**

hash clusters. If there is a one-to-one mapping between hash keys and data rows (like a primary key or unique key index), Oracle is able to locate a single row without scanning all rows in the block." As a result, hash clusters should only be used in very specific circumstances. But under those circumstances, hash clusters provide high performance access to Oracle data.

Oracle9i External Tables

Seasoned data warehouse administrators know that getting data out of the data warehouse is not the only challenging issue they must address. Extracting, transforming and loading data into the data warehouse can also be quite formidable (and quite expensive) tasks.

Before we begin our discussion on data warehousing, we need to understand that the data warehouse always contains data from external sources. The data is extracted from the source systems, transformed from operational data to decision support data using transformation logic, and ultimately, loaded into the data warehouse tables. This process of extracting data from source systems and populating the data warehouse is called Extraction, Transformation and Loading or ETL. Shops deploying data warehouses have the options of purchasing third-party ETL tools or writing scripts and programs to perform the transformation process manually.

Before Oracle9i, the most common methods of manually performing complex transformations were:

- The extracted data would be loaded into staging tables in the data warehouse. The staged data would be transformed in the database and then used as input to programs that updated the permanent data warehouse tables.

- The data would be transformed in flat files stored outside of the database. When the transformation process was complete, the data would be loaded into the data warehouse.

Oracle9i introduces external tables, which provide a mechanism to view data stored in external sources as if it were a table in the database. This ability to read external data provides a more straightforward method of loading and transforming data from external sources. Administrators no longer need to reserve space inside the database for staging tables or write external programs to transform the data outside of the database environment. By making it no longer necessary to stage data in the Oracle database, Oracle9i's external tables have essentially streamlined the ETL function by merging the transformation and loading processes.

External tables in Oracle are read-only and cannot have indexes built upon them. Their main use is a data source for more traditional Oracle table structures. Data warehouse administrators are able to use the CREATE TABLE AS SELECT.... and the INSERT INTO.....AS SELECT statements to populate Oracle tables using the external source as input.

Much of the data validation and cleansing that occurs during the ETL process requires access to existing data stored in the data warehouse. Since the external table data is viewed by the database as ordinary table data, SQL, PL/SQL and Java can be used to perform the data transformations. Joins, sorts, referential integrity verification, ID lookups and advanced string manipulations can be performed in the database environment. In addition, advanced SQL statements such as UPSERT and multi-table INSERT statements allow data to be easily integrated into the warehouse environment. The power of the database can be fully utilized to facilitate the transformation process.

External table definitions do not describe how the data is stored externally, rather they describe how the external data is to be presented to the Oracle database engine. Let's take a quick look at an external table definition:

```
CREATE TABLE empxt
(empno        NUMBER(4),
ename         VARCHAR2(10),
job            VARCHAR2(9),
mgr           NUMBER(4),
hiredate      VARCHAR2(20),
sal            NUMBER(7,2),
comm          NUMBER(7,2),
deptno        NUMBER(2))
ORGANIZATION EXTERNAL
(TYPE ORACLE_LOADER
DEFAULT DIRECTORY dat_dir
ACCESS PARAMETERS
(records delimited by newline
badfile bad_dir:'empxt%a_%p.bad'
logfile log_dir:'empxt%a_%p.log'
fields terminated by ','
missing field values are null
(empno, ename, job, mgr,
hiredate, sal, comm, deptno))
LOCATION ('empxt1.dat', 'empxt2.dat'))
REJECT LIMIT UNLIMITED;
```

Most of the above table's definition should be familiar to us. However, a few parameters warrant further investigation:

- ORGANIZATION EXTERNAL – Designates that the table's data resides in an external location

- TYPE – Indicates the access driver. The access driver is the API that interprets the external data for the database. If you do not specify TYPE in the table's definition, Oracle uses the default access driver, *oracle_loader*.

- DEFAULT DIRECTORY – specifies one or more default directory objects that correspond to directories on the file system where the external data resides. Default directories are able to contain both source data and output files (logs, bad files, discard files, etc.). The directory objects that refer to the directories on the file system must already be created with the CREATE DIRECTORY SQL statement. In addition, read access must be granted to directory objects containing the source data and write access must be granted to all directories that are to contain output files (BAD_DIR, LOG_DIR). Users wanting access to external table data must be granted the appropriate security on the directory objects as well as the table.

- ACCESS PARAMETERS – Assigns values to access driver parameters.

- BADFILE, LOGFILE –Oracle load utility output files.

- LOCATION – Specifies the location for each external data source. The Oracle server does not interpret this clause. The access driver specified interprets this information in the context of the external data.

- PARALLEL (not specified) - Enables parallel query processing on the external data source.

Oracle9i External Tables

Oracle9i external tables provide great benefits to warehouse environments by combining the transformation and external data access processes. Oracle calls the process "pipelining" and describes it as "a whole new model for loading and transforming external data."

There is a wealth of information available on Oracle9i external tables. Instead of providing you with an in-depth description of how to implement and administer Oracle9i external tables, please refer to Dave Moore's excellent article in DBAZINE titled "External Tables in Oracle9i." His suggestion to use the external table feature to use SQL statements to search the database alert log is a GREAT idea!

ALTER TABLE MOVE Statement

If you are using Oracle8i or later releases, don't use the Export/Import utilities to change initial storage settings for a table, defragment it or move it to a different tablespace. Oracle8i introduced the ALTER TABLE MOVE statement that allows administrators to move data from one tablespace to another and change initial storage settings while the table is online.

ALTER COLUMN RENAME

Another long-awaited enhancement has finally arrived! Administrators are finally able to rename columns using a simple SQL statement. The new ALTER TABLE RENAME COLUMN statement is introduced in Oracle9i Release 2 to provide column-renaming functionality. No longer are administrators required to drop and reload tables or use the *dbms_redefinition* stored procedure (introduced in Oracle 9i Release 1) to rename columns in Oracle. The example below shows the new statement in action:

```
ALTER TABLE foot.emp RENAME COLUMN salry to salary;
```

On-Line Table Reorganizations

Oracle9i allows DBAs to perform complex table redefinitions on-line. Administrators now have the capability to change column names and datatypes, manipulate data, add and drop columns and partition tables while the table is being accessed by on-line transactions (for a complete list of changes, please refer to the Oracle9i Administration Guide). This new feature provides significant benefits over more traditional methods of altering tables that require the object to be taken off-line during the redefinition process. Oracle9i provides a set of procedures stored in the PL/SQL package DBMS_REDFINITION as the mechanism to perform on-line redefinitions.

Most tables in Oracle can be redefined. The Oracle9*i* Administration Guide provides a listing of table specifications that will prohibit a table from being redefined on-line. For example, one requirement is that the table being redefined must have a primary key. Oracle9i provides a procedure that will check the table to determine if it can be redefined. The example below shows the table SCOTT.SOURCE_EMP being checked to determine if it meets the on-line redefinition criteria:
EXEC dbms_redefinition.can_redef_table ('SCOTT', 'SOURCE_EMP');

Administrators create an empty work table in the same schema as the table to be redefined. This work table is created with all of the desired attributes and will become the new table when the redefinition is executed. The two table definitions below show our source table (SCOTT.SOURCE_EMP) and the table containing our desired attributes (SCOTT.WORK_EMP):

```
CREATE TABLE scott.source_emp
(empno NUMBER(4) PRIMARY KEY,
ename VARCHAR2(10),
job VARCHAR2(9),
mgr NUMBER(4),
hiredate DATE,
sal NUMBER(7, 2),
comm NUMBER(7, 2),
deptno NUMBER(2));

create table scott.work_emp
(enum NUMBER PRIMARY KEY,
lname VARCHAR2(20),
new_col TIMESTAMP,
salary  NUMBER));
```

After the redefinition process is complete, SCOTT.WORK_EMP will become the new SCOTT.SOURCE_EMP table and SCOTT.SOURCE_EMP will become SCOTT.WORK_EMP. The tables are in effect "swapped" during the final phase of transformation.

The next step is to transfer the data from the SCOTT.SOURCE_EMP table to SCOTT.WORK_EMP using the DBMS_REDEFINITION.START_REDEF_TABLE procedure. The step also links the two tables together for the remainder of the redefinition process. Administrators code column mappings and data modifications during this step to transform the data. The statement below shows the SCOTT.SOURCE_EMP data being manipulated as it is being transferred to the SCOTT.WORK_EMP table:

```
EXEC dbms_redefinition.start_redef_table
('SCOTT', 'SOURCE_EMP', 'WORK_EMP', 'EMPNO ENUM, ENAM LNAME,
SAL*3 SALARY');
```

The above redefinition statement multiplies the SALARY column by three and renames columns EMPNO to ENUM and ENAM to LNAM. The work table also has a new column added (NEW_COL) and does not have column definitions for JOB, MGR, HIREDATE, COMM and DEPTNO.

Triggers, indexes, constraints and grants can now be created on the work table. Referential constraints must be created using the DISABLE option. All triggers, indexes, constraints and grants replace those on the source table being redefined.

The final step of the redefinition process is to execute DBMS_REDEFINITION.FINISH_REDEF_TABLE, which performs the following functions:

- The work table becomes the new source table. The new source table's definition includes all grants, indexes, constraints and triggers created on the work table during the transformation process.

- All referential integrity constraints created on the work table are enabled.

- The source table becomes the new work table. All grants, indexes, constraints and triggers that were on the old source table are also transferred. Referential integrity constraints on the new work table are disabled.

On-Line Table Reorganizations **139**

- All DML statements applied to the old source table during the redefinition process are transferred to the work (new source) table.
- The tables are only locked for the length of time it takes to perform the table name "swap."

PL/SQL procedures that access the table being redefined are invalidated. They may remain invalidated if the redefinition process has changed the table structure in such a way that they can no longer successfully access the table data.

During the time period between the executions of START_REDEF_TABLE and FINISH_REDEF_TABLE, Oracle9i saves all DML changes being applied to the source table. These recorded changes are applied to the work table during the final step of the transformation process. The number of stored changes that need to be applied has a direct affect on the length of time it takes FINISH_REDEF_TABLE to execute. A large number of changes being applied to the source table during the redefinition process may cause the FINISH_REDEF_TABLE step to become quite "lengthy."

Administrators are able to execute the DBMS_REDEFINITION.SYNC_INTERIM_TABLE procedure to periodically synchronize the source and work tables during the period between START_REDEF_TABLE and FINISH_REDEF_TABLE. Periodically synchronizing the tables reduces the number of stored changes that need to be applied to the work table and the amount of time it takes FINISH_REDEF to execute.

Oracle9i supplies DBMS_REDEFINITION.ABORT_REDEF_TABLE that can be used to cancel the redefinition process. Administrators are able to abort the process at any time between the executions of START_REDEF_TABLE and FINISH_REDEF_TABLE.

PCTFREE and PCTUSED

If you don't have enough information to make an educated guess on these parameters, don't make an uneducated one. Select the default values and monitor for chained rows by using the LIST CHAINED ROWS option in the ANALYZE statement.

Clustering Data in Tables

Before clusters, Oracle didn't have a mechanism to sort data in a table to match the order of a particular index. But clusters can be difficult to tune and administer, yet they do increase performance in certain (limited) circumstances. If you can't (or don't want to) use clusters, try this option. If the application always access the table by the same column or the table is always joined to other tables by the same column, consider sorting the data on that column before loading. Static tables are the easiest to sort, but I have seen administrators in OLTP systems pump data out of tables into flat files, sort the records in the proper order and reload them using the load utility on a regular basis.

Merging Tables to Increase Query Performance

If you constantly join two or more tables together in an application, merge them into one table. It's called "de-normalizing for performance" (your data administrator make call it and you other things). It's simple and it works.

The Oracle Database Fundamentals I (1Z0-031) certification test will contain a few questions on Oracle tables. Test candidates should know:

- The specifications used to create and modify an Oracle table
- The differences between an Oracle table and an Index-Organized table (IOT)
- Datatypes
- ROWID formats
- Row structure
- Database constraints
    - Constraint states (validate, novalidate)
    - Immediate and deferred constraints
    - Primary and unique key enforcement
    - Enabling and disabling constrains
    - Constraint types
        - Check
        - Primary key
        - Unique key

- Not Null
- Online reorganizations
- Oracle9i external tables

How Many Indexes Can I Build?

This subject has always been a matter for great debate. The DBA must balance the performance of SELECT statements with their DML (INSERT, UPDATE and DELETE) counterparts. SELECT statements that access non-indexed columns often suffer from poor performance. Conversely, if you have too many indexes on a particular table, DML statements may be adversely affected.

The DBA must take the business requirements, application processing workload and workload scheduling into consideration when determining how many indexes to build. If you compare the performance improvements an index makes on a SELECT statement to the negative affect it has on DML statements, you will find that the benefits of building the index far outweigh the performance drawbacks. Indexes on columns in the WHERE clause of SELECT statements can reduce query times by minutes and even hours. The creation of additional indexes may add a few seconds to most on-line transactions that execute DML statements. Additional indexes will have the greatest negative impact on statements that process a large number of rows. The more rows that are inserted, deleted or changed, the greater the negative impact will be. Traditionally, programs that process large volumes of rows are scheduled to execute during off-hours.

The DBA must also consider the needs of the business. What process is more important to the business unit – getting the data in or getting the data out? Who complains the most? The business user that must wait minutes (or hours) for their transaction to retrieve data or the business user that is waiting an extra few seconds for their update transaction to complete.

The DBA will need to find out how much time the additional indexes add to programs that process large volumes of rows. In addition, the DBA must determine when these programs run. If they run at night or do not require high-performance, consider building the index. Transaction concurrency must also be taken into consideration. The more columns in the indexes that are changed, the longer the index-entry will be locked.

If the transaction update performance requirements are excessive (dot com applications are one example), keep the number of indexes to a minimum. A good recommendation is to build a set of tables that have no indexes for lighting-fast update performance and move the data to historical tables (with proper indexing) during off-hours to increase retrieval performance.

Parameters that Impact Index Usage

The following parameters influence the Oracle cost-based optimizer to favor or not favor index access:

- *optimizer_mode* = first_rows - The optimizer chooses the best plan for fast delivery of the first few rows. More often than not, that access path will include an index.

- *optimizer_mode* = all_rows – The optimizer chooses the best plan for fast delivery of all of the rows that queries return. This usually means that the optimizer will favor full table scans over index access.

- *optimizer_index_cost_adj* = xxxx – This WORKS! This parameter lets you tune the optimizer to be more or less index "friendly." It allows the administrators to influence the optimizer to make it more or less prone to selecting an index access path over a full table scan.

  The default for this parameter is 100 percent. This setting tells the optimizer to evaluate index access paths at the regular cost. Any other value makes the optimizer evaluate the access path at that percentage of the regular cost. For example, a setting of 50 makes the index access path look half as expensive as normal.

- *optimizer_index_caching* = xxxx - Lets you adjust the behavior of cost-based optimization to favor indexes and nested loops joins over merge scan joins (which are often associated with full table scans). You set this parameter to a value between 0 and 100 to indicate the percentage of the index blocks the optimizer should assume are in the cache. Setting this parameter to a higher value makes nested loops joins (and the indexes used to probe them) look less expensive to the optimizer.

Index-Only Access

Most DBAs know that creating indexes on columns contained in the WHERE clause of a statement increases query performance. So we can assume that creating an index on all of the columns in the WHERE clause should really increase performance. How about including every column in the statement in the index? An old DBA trick is to include columns from the SELECT clause in a statement to the end of the columns in the index (see Figure 7). If all of the columns that were in the WHERE clause were also in the index, the query's access path would be index-only access. With index-only access, there is no need to go to the table to retrieve column data. All of the columns accessed in the statement are contained in the index structure.

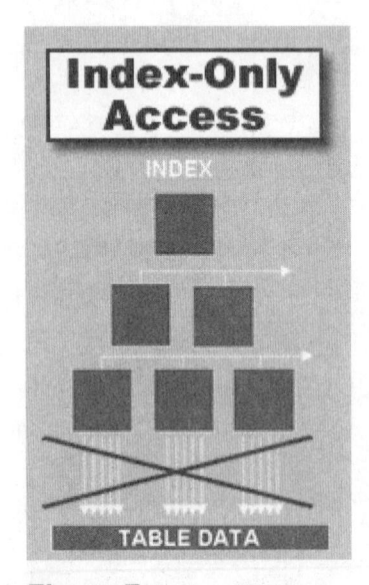

Figure 7 *Index-Only Access*

If the query being tuned doesn't select many columns and you have all of the columns in the WHERE clause in the index, consider index-only access. Add all of the columns in the SELECT clause to the end of the column list in the index to achieve lightning fast data access. The examples below show you how to implement index only access:

```
SELECT part_name, part_location
FROM gm.part
WHERE part_id = 50;

CREATE INDEX gm.part_index
ON gm.part(part_id, part_name, part_location);
```

The example above shows a query that selects part_name and part_location from the gm.part table. The index gm.part_index is created on part_id AND part_name and part_location to obtain an index-only access path.

How many columns can you add? I have added up to 7 or 8 columns to the index structure and have seen query performance improve dramatically. The number of columns is not the critical factor, column length is. DML statements that insert and update column values will take longer due to the increase in the number of columns in the index structure. You need to figure out what is more important to your application, reducing data query times or retaining the performance of DML statements.

Index Rebuilds

In releases prior to Oracle8i, the CREATE INDEX and ALTER INDEX REBUILD commands lock the table with a Share Table Lock (S). No DML operations are permitted on the base table. Oracle version 8.1 introduced a new REBUILD command keyword, ONLINE. If the ONLINE key word is included as part of the CREATE INDEX or ALTER INDEX....REBUILD commands, the table is locked with a Row Share Table Lock (RS). Users will be able to continue to access the table as normal except for any DDL operations. DML operations are permitted.

When the ONLINE keyword is specified as a part of an CREATE INDEX or ALTER INDEX....REBUILD command, a temporary journal table is created to record changes made to the base table. The journal is an IOT (Index Organized Table) table type. Oracle merges the changes entered in the journal at the end of the index build process. This merge process is performed while the table is still online. Oracle may make multiple passes over the journal table to process previously locked rows.

Index Coalesce vs Index Rebuild

Space freed in a table because of row deletes becomes immediately available for reuse. This is not the case for the associated index entries. The index entries pointing to the rows are marked as deleted, but the space consumed by the index entries cannot be reused until the index structure is compressed. In volatile OLTP environments, you may have indexes that have only a few active entries per block. The results are inefficient B-Tree index structures and poor performance. The ANALYZE INDEX ... VALIDATE STRUCTURE statement can be used to identify the number of deleted leaf entries in the index structure.

Oracle8i offers you two ways to compress an index structure. The ALTER INDEX ... REBUILD statement is used to reorganize or compact an existing index or to change its storage characteristics. The REBUILD statement uses the existing index as the basis for the new one. As a result, the index will consume twice as much space during the rebuild process. All index storage statements are supported, such as STORAGE (for extent allocation), TABLESPACE (to move the index to a new tablespace), and INITRANS (to change the initial number of entries).

ALTER INDEX ... REBUILD is faster than dropping and re-creating an index, because this statement uses the fast full scan feature. It reads all index blocks using multiblock I/O then discards the branch blocks. A further advantage of this approach is that the old index is still available for queries while the rebuild is in progress. The ONLINE keyword specifies that DML operations on the table or partition be allowed during the rebuild process.

The ALTER INDEX.....COALESCE statement instructs Oracle to merge the contents of index blocks where possible to free blocks for reuse. The index structure itself is not affected (see Figure 8). Oracle works within the branches to remove the deleted leaf entries and compress remaining rows into the smallest number of blocks possible.

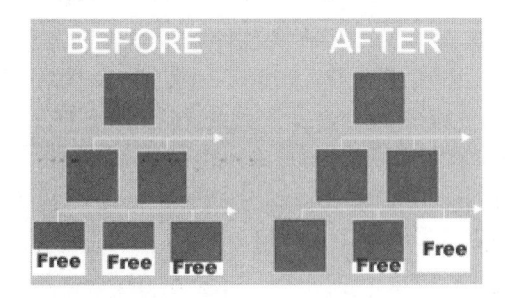

Figure 8 *Index structure*

The following information will help you choose which compress method to use:

Index Coalesce vs Index Rebuild

- REBUILD can move an index from one tablespace to another. COALESCE can't.

- REBUILD takes longer and requires more space. COALESCE is much quicker because it consumes less resources.

- REBUILD creates a new B-Tree structure and shrinks the height if possible. COALESCE works within the same branch of the tree, will not move entries to other branches and will not shrink the height.

- REBUILD enables you to quickly change storage and tablespace parameters without having to drop the original index. COALESCE can't.

- If you shrink the height of an index, it will be faster than if the index was coalesced.

Function-Based Indexes

Generally, the fastest way to access Oracle data is with an index. Oracle's bitmap and B-Tree indexes are designed to provide complementary performance functionality. While standard B-tree indexes perform best with key columns containing a high number of different values (good selectivity), bitmap indexes work best with columns that have a limited number (poor selectivity) of possible values.

Administrators supporting large data stores use partitioned indexes to decompose large index structures into smaller, more manageable pieces called index partitions. Oracle places index data in the separate index partitions based on the index's partitioning key. The partitioning key of an index must include one or more of the columns that define the index.

Oracle8i solved an indexing problem that has been affecting database performance for close to a decade. Before Oracle8i, any SQL statement that contained a function or expression on the columns being searched on in the WHERE clause could not use an index. For example, the statement:

```
SELECT emp_lname FROM employee WHERE salary + commission >
100000;
```

An index would not be used. A full table scan would be required to retrieve the desired result set. We now know that we are able to use B-tree and bitmap indexes to speed query performance. In Oracle8i, we are able to build both bitmap and B-tree indexes on columns containing the aforementioned functions or expressions. A function-based index precomputes the value of the function or expression and stores it in the index. The following index could be used to increase performance of the query:

```
CREATE INDEX sal_comm on emp (salary + commission);
```

Bitmap Indexes

A traditional B-Tree (balanced tree) index stores the key values and pointers in an inverted tree structure. The key to good B-Tree index performance is to build the index on columns having what Oracle describes as "good selectivity". Oracle is able to quickly bypass rows that do not meet the search criteria when searching through indexes built on columns having a high degree of selectivity.

Conversely, bitmap indexes perform better when the selectivity of an index is poor. A bitmap index is a set of multiple bitmap structures containing a series of bits (see figure 9). If the bit is on, the corresponding row has that value. If it is off, the row does not. The first index entry of each bitmap structure contains a row address that identifies where the first row can be found in the table. All of the remaining entries are then found positionally, that is they are identified by how many entries they are from the starting entry in the bitmap. If you are looking for all of the rows that have a gender = "male", Oracle would search the bits looking for the "on" value to find the rows.

Bitmap Indexes

gender =	male	female
Row 1	1	0
Row 2	0	1
Row 3	0	1
Row 4	1	0
Row 5	1	0

Figure 9: Bitmap index.

The fewer different values a bitmap index contains, the better it will perform. Bitmap indexes, in certain situations, can provide impressive performance benefits. Bitmap indexes are most appropriate for complex and ad-hoc queries that contain lengthy WHERE clauses on columns that have a limited number of different values (poor selectivity).

Optimizer and Bitmap Indexes

The optimizer can be stubborn at times. It can be particularly stubborn when you want it to choose a bitmap index for an access path. A single bitmap index may not be chosen at all. The optimizer will be more inclined to choose bitmap indexes as an access path if it can use multiple bitmap indexes simultaneously. If you want Oracle to choose bitmap indexes as an access path, build a lot of them or use hints.

Concurrency and Bitmap Indexes

Anyone accustomed to database programming understands the potential for concurrency problems. When one application program tries to read data that is in the process of being changed by another, the DBMS must forbid access until the modification is complete in order to ensure data integrity. Each entry in a B-Tree index entry contains a single ROWID. When the index entry is locked during an update, a single row is affected. A bitmap index entry can potentially contain a range of ROWIDs. When Oracle locks the bitmap index entry, the entire range of ROWIDs is also locked. The number of ROWIDs contained in the range affects the level of concurrency. As ROWIDs increase in the bitmap segment, the level of concurrency decreases.

When to Use Bitmap Indexes

Locking issues affect data manipulation operations in Oracle. As a result, a bitmap index is not a good choice for OLTP applications that have a high level of concurrent INSERT, DELETE and UPDATE operations. Concurrency is usually not an issue in a data-warehousing environment where the data is maintained by large loads, inserts and updates. Bitmap index maintenance is deferred until the end of any large DML operation. If 100 rows are inserted into a table, the inserted rows are placed into a sort buffer and the updates of all 100 index entries are applied as a group. As a result, bitmap indexes are appropriate for most decision support applications (even those that have bulk updates applied on a regular basis).

Mass updates, inserts and delete will run faster if you drop the bitmap indexes, execute the DML and recreate the bitmap indexes when the DML completes. Run timings using the straight DML and compare it to the total time consumed by the drop bitmap index/execute DML/recreate bitmap index process.

DBAs must also take column cardinality into consideration when determining the potential performance benefits of bitmap indexes. The higher the index's cardinality, the larger the index becomes. If a table containing GENDER (values 'M' and 'F') and HAIR_COLOR (values 'BLOND', 'BLACK', 'BRUNETTE', 'REDHEAD') columns contains 1 million rows, the bitmap index on GENDER would require 2 million entries and the bitmap index on HAIR_COLOR would require 4 million entries.

Bitmap vs B-Tree

We just learned that standard B-tree indexes are most effective for columns containing a high number of different values (good selectivity) and bitmap indexes are most appropriate for columns with a limited number (poor selectivity) of possible values. Where is the selectivity cutoff point? What is that magic number of different values when a bitmap or a B-tree is no longer considered to be a viable indexing option? There are many variables (number of rows, column cardinality, query composition, update frequency) that must be considered when determining the potential performance benefits of bitmap and B-tree indexes. The only definitive method of determining the potential performance benefits of bitmap and B-tree indexes is to create them and monitor the application's performance.

I've seen B-Tree indexes bring back 25% of the rows faster than table scans and have seen bitmap indexes with a couple of dozen different values perform flawlessly. Remember that "rules of thumb" are just general recommendations. Benchmark testing is the ONLY way to determine if a new index will increase query performance.

Indexing Hints Tips and Tricks

Some key points on indexing:
- If you are using the cost-based optimizer, run ANALYZE on all tables in the query. Oracle doesn't like to make assumptions.

- Index on join columns that have the proper selectivity.
- Always index on foreign key columns (and make sure the columns in the index and the columns in the foreign key match exactly). If you don't, two things will happen when you execute DML against the parent table:
    - Oracle will have to scan the child table that has a negative impact on performance.
    - Oracle will hold a table level lock on the child table that has a negative impact on concurrency.
- The leading column of the index must be used in the WHERE clause for the index to be chosen (except when using fast full scan).
- Index column order - put columns most often used in queries in front of columns not used as frequently.
- The inner table of a hash or sort merge join cannot be probed solely using an index on the join columns.
- The inner table of a nested loop can be probed by an index on the join column, but the outer table can't.
- Create indexes on columns used in local (non-join) predicates on the outer table of a nested loop join. Index local predicates to influence the outer and inner table selection in nested loop joins.
- Use histograms on skewed data.
- If the query being tuned doesn't SELECT a lot of columns and you have all of the columns in the WHERE clause in the index, consider INDEX ONLY access. Add all of the columns in the

SELECT clause to the end of the column list in the index to achieve lightning fast data access.

- Consider creating multiple, single column indexes on a table to achieve multiple index access.

- Primary and unique key indexes seem to have a greater chance of being used than other indexes. You may have index-only access with another index, but you will probably be forced to use a hint to get Oracle to use it.

- Indexes can't be used when Oracle is forced to perform implicit datatype conversion.

- Subselects and views may cause the optimizer to rewrite the SQL which could result in indexes not being used.

- Modifications to the column side of the query prevent an index from being used on the column being modified. Function-based indexes can be used to prevent table scans

- Use the EXISTS function instead of the IN function when tables in the subselect portion of the query are small.

Index Monitoring

Determining if an index will increase performance is a pretty straightforward process. The administrator is focusing their tuning efforts on a particular table or query and is able to gather the specific information necessary to assist in the decision making process.

Dropping unused indexes is also an important part of application tuning. Indexes force Oracle to occur additional I/O every time a row is inserted or deleted into the table they are built upon. Every update of the table's columns incurs additional I/O to all indexes defined on those columns. Unused indexes also waste space and add unnecessary administrative complexity.

Determining if indexes were being used in releases prior to Oracle9i was a time consuming and error-prone process. EXPLAIN plan and trace output could be used but there was no single mechanism that monitored index usage at the database level.

Oracle9i simplifies the index usage monitoring process by providing the ALTER INDEX......... MONITOR USAGE command. To successfully start or stop a monitoring session, the user must be logged on as the schema owner of the index. The statement below turns monitoring on for the index SCOTT.EMPIDX while the second statement ends the monitoring session:

```
ALTER INDEX scott.empidx MONITORING USAGE;
ALTER INDEX scott.empidx NOMONITORING USAGE;
```

The *v$object_usage* table can then be accessed to determine if the index was used during the monitoring session. When the session is started, Oracle clears the information in *v$object_usage* for the index being monitored and enters a new start time identifying when the index monitoring session started. After the index monitoring session is concluded, the USED column in the *v$object_usage* table will contain the value 'YES' if the index was used during the monitoring session and the value 'NO' if it was not.

The Oracle Database Fundamentals I (1Z0-031) and the Oracle Database Performance Tuning (1Z0-033) certification tests will have numerous questions on Oracle indexes. Test candidates should understand:

- The basic structure of B-Tree and Bitmap indexes
- The syntax used to create and modify Oracle indexes
- Comparison of Bitmap vs. B-Tree. Know which index to use based on application processing requirements.
- Rebuilding vs. coalescing
- The impact indexing has on query performance
- How to activate index monitoring
- Function-based indexes
- Reverse key indexes
- Parameters that affect index usage

Conclusion

This chapter provided a great deal of information on Oracle database objects. The Oracle Concepts Guide and the Administrator's Guide are excellent manuals to turn to for more information. The Concepts Guide will help you better understand the objects themselves while the Administrator's Guide will help you to administer them effectively. Some of the key topics discussed in this chapter are:

- Know what database you are administering. Using *glogin.sql*, *login.sql* and UNIX prompts to display the database name will prevent you from making changes to the wrong database.

- Choosing the correct initial blocksize is critical. Select it wisely. It can't be changed without dropping and recreating the database.

- Don't use the EXPORT/IMPORT utilities to transfer databases to other destinations. Use datafile copies and the ALTER DATABASE BACKUP CONTROLFILE TO TRACE; statement to quickly and easily migrate large databases.

- Tablespace partitioning and query parallelism are essential components of any Oracle Data Warehouse.

- Oracle9i provides administrators with a wealth of different tablespace options. Use locally managed tablespaces and allow Oracle to manage extent sizes and block freespace by specifying AUTOALLOCATE and SEGMENT SPACE MANAGEMENT AUTO, respectively.

- Oracle9i offers system managed undo segments. The chapter in the Oracle8i DBA I class on rollback segments was over 45 pages long while the chapter in the Oracle9i DBA I class is only 15 pages. What used to take instructors an afternoon to teach now takes under an hour. What better testament to their ease of administration? Use system managed undo segments to simplify the management of transaction before images.

- If you see "CHECKPOINT NOT COMPLETE" messages in the alert log, resize your online redo logs to increase performance dramatically.

In the next chapter we discuss one of my favorite topics, backup and recovery. Being able to successfully recover is a job requirement for all DBAs. It won't make any difference how well you can tune a database or design an application; if you can't recover the database when required, your reputation (and job security) will suffer.

Oracle Backup and Recovery

CHAPTER 6

Recovering an Oracle database is a wonderfully complex task. Data files, log files, control files, full backups, hot backups and point-in-time recoveries all combine to make many administrators lie awake nights thinking about whether their databases can be easily recovered (or not). Oracle contains many features that remove much of the burden from the administrator and places it where it belongs; squarely on the shoulders of the Oracle server. The next few sections will provide some useful information on the Oracle backup and recovery process.

It's the Little Things That Bite You

Most botched recoveries can be attributed to human error. Make sure all tapes have proper retention periods, verify that all backups are executing correctly and run test recoveries on a regular basis. Don't let missing tapes or backups cause you to lose data. You don't want to hear UNIX support say "the retention on that tape was supposed to be how long?" in the middle of a recovery. COMMUNICATE with others that are responsible for all other pieces of the recovery "pie" (system admins, operators) on a regular basis to ensure you have everything you need to recover a crashed database.

Keep Your Skills Sharp

Don't let your recovery skills get rusty. Create one database that you and your fellow administrators can trash on a regular basis. Take turns and make a game out of it. DBAs can be pretty creative when causing problems for others when it's all in fun. Spend dedicated time keeping your recovery skills sharp. If you are a senior-level DBA, make sure you keep the junior folks on their toes. A staff that has up-to-date recovery experience means less calls to you at 2AM.

RELAX and Plan Your Attack

When you are notified of a database failure, take a deep breath and relax. Don't immediately begin to paste the database back together without a plan. Create a recovery plan, put it on paper, have others review it if you can, and then execute it. You shouldn't be trying to determine what the next step is in the middle of the recovery process.

Don't Be Afraid to Ask Others

I have 16 years of experience using Oracle and have done my fair share of database recoveries (5 databases in 4 days is my current record. A bad batch of disks was the cause.). If possible, I still have others review my recovery strategy and recovery steps during the recovery process. Don't be afraid to ask others and don't be afraid of calling Oracle support if you have to. That's what they get paid by your company to do – support you. Don't make a database unrecoverable by "guessing." I once viewed over 100 different commands in an alert log after a botched recovery performed by a junior DBA. An ego that was too big to allow that person to ask questions created a database that was unrecoverable.

Instance Recovery and the Oracle Synchronization Process

Oracle instructors often discuss the concept of Oracle data being "out of synch" because the DWBR and LGRW processes act independently. Let's take an in-depth look at how data gets "out of synch" in Oracle and how Oracle gets itself back into shape when it needs to.

There are two memory constructs, two background processes and one storage structure that we need to have a firm understanding of before we continue:

- Data buffer cache - memory area used to store blocks read from the data files.

- Log buffer - memory used to contain before and after images of changed data. Please note the words before and after.

- DBWR background process - writes dirty buffers from the data buffer cache to the data files.

- LGWR background process - writes dirty buffers from the redo log buffer to the redo log files.

- Rollback/Undo segments - used to hold before images for transaction recovery, instance recovery and read consistency. Every transaction in Oracle that changes data will write a before image of that data to the rollback segment. If the transaction fails, or the instance fails, the before images stored in the rollback segment are used to put the database back into a transaction consistent state.

When a user process (started by SQL*PLUS, Forms, Reports, OEM, application program, etc.) connects to a database, Oracle starts a server process that performs steps to complete the user process's requests. The server process is responsible for checking the data buffer cache to determine if the data the user process is looking for is available in the cache. If the data is not contained in the data buffer cache, it is the server process's responsibility to read the desired data block from a file on disk and place it in the data buffer cache. If the user process wants to change the data, the server process records a before and after image of the data being changed in the data buffer cache and places it into the redo log buffer cache.

The Oracle Database Fundamentals I (1Z0-031) and the Oracle Database Fundamentals II (1Z0-032) certification tests will have questions on the Oracle synchronization process. Test candidates should have a firm understanding of all of the activities performed and objects used during synchronization.

Uncommitted Data on the Data Files

If the user's server process is unable to find a free data buffer, DBWR is notified to flush changed data buffers to their corresponding data files. There are many different criteria that cause the buffer to be "force flushed." It is interesting to note that DBWR makes no distinction between committed and uncommitted data. The data buffers being flushed may contain both committed and uncommitted changes. This could result in Oracle having uncommitted and committed data blocks on the data files. A key point is that before a flush of changed data buffers to disk occurs, DBWR will signal LGWR to write all before images of uncommitted blocks in the section being flushed. This process ensures that all before images of uncommitted data changes can be retrieved from the redo log file during a recovery.

Committed Data Not On the Data Files

When a transaction commits, the server process places a commit record in the log buffer and tells LGWR to perform a contiguous write of all the redo log buffer entries up to and including the COMMIT record to the redo log files (not the data files!). Oracle is now able to guarantee that the changes will not be lost even if there is an instance failure. Please note that the DBWR flushes the dirty data buffers independently and this can occur either before or after the commit. This could result in Oracle having committed data on the redo log files but not on the data files.

The Synchronization Process

If a failure occurs and the instance terminates abnormally, Oracle must restore the database to a transaction consistent state just prior to the failure. The database must remove all uncommitted data from the data files and replay all changes committed and recorded in the redo log files but not recorded on the data files (remember that a commit forces LGWR to flush, not DBWR). Oracle restores the database to a transaction consistent state using roll forward and roll backward processes.

Roll Forward Phase

During this phase, DBWR writes both committed and uncommitted data from the redo log files to the data files. The purpose of the roll forward is to apply all changes recorded in the log files to the corresponding data blocks. Rollback/undo segments are populated during the roll forward phase. A rollback/undo segment entry is added if an uncommitted data block is found on the data files and no undo entry exists in the rollback/undo segment. At the end of this phase, all committed data is in the data files, although uncommitted data may still exist. The database is then opened to allow user access to database data.

Roll Backward Phase

Oracle removes the uncommitted data by using the rollback/undo segments populated during the roll forward phase or prior to the crash. Blocks are rolled back when requested by the Oracle server or a user's server process, depending on which process requests the block first. The database is therefore available even while the roll backward phase is executing. Only those data blocks that are actively participating in the rollback are not available. Total data synchronization has now occurred.

Exports and Recovery

A common misconception is that a database can be recovered up to the current point-in-time by: recreating the database, recreating the data with a full database import and using the logs to roll forward. That recovery methodology will not work. Exports work within the data files and don't change the file headers. The database will only be consistent to the point in time when the Export file was created.

V$RECOVERFILE

Query the *v$recoverfile* table to determine how many files are missing or corrupted before you have them restored. The operators will like you much better and the recovery process will be a lot faster if you restore all of the files that have been lost at the same time.

Watch the NOLOGGING Option

The NOLOGGING option is great for performance but it tends to complicate current point-in-time recoveries (to say the least). If you load or insert data using the NOLOGGING option and you don't immediately take a backup, you're asking for trouble. If you have to execute a complete database recovery, the database will be out of synch. Here's the reason. If transactions that depend on the data loaded or inserted using the NOLOGGING option were executed after the NOLOGGING statements were run, they are accessing data that's not there! Take a backup after a NOLOGGING statement or utility execution.

Striped File Systems

If mirroring is not used, exercise caution when placing redo logs and/or control files on the same disk stripes as data files. If you lose any disk contained in the stripe, you also lose your ability to recover the database to the current point-in-time. Call me old-fashioned, I still try to sneak a copy of the control files and redo logs on a non-striped drive. If the stripe containing the other copies becomes unusable, the copies on the non-stripe disk are available to use as input to a forward recovery. I just can't bring myself to place all of my multiplexed redo log files and control files on the same stripe (whether that stripe is mirrored or not).

Data Files and Redo Logs

If mirroring is not used, don't place redo logs and data files on the same disk. Once again, you may lose your ability to recover the database to the current point-in-time.

Redo Log and Control File Multiplexing

Make sure your redo log groups have two or more members in each group with each member being on a different disk drive. Multiple copies of the control file should also be maintained on different disks. There should be a very limited number of reasons why you have to recover a database due to the loss of all members of a redo log group or control file set.

OCOPY for Windows

Oracle on Windows provides the OCOPY command to circumvent Windows file locking problems. Use OCOPY instead of the COPY command when performing hot backups on Windows.

Hot Backup Scripts for Windows

The following scripts automate a complete hot database backup of an Oracle8i database on Windows. The traditional caveats can be applied. It can be changed easily to fit your specific environment. It backs up the entire database, so it may not be the best script to use for large environments. In addition, watch connecting to a tool by hard coding the account and password in the script. The first script to execute should contain the following commands:

ntbackup.cmd sets the *oracle_sid* and calls *generate_back.sql*. *generate_back.sql* reads the data dictionary and writes the backup commands to *runback.sql*. *ntbackup.cmd* then performs the actual backup by running *runback.sql*.

NTBACKUP.CMD

```
set ORACLE_SID=orcl
plus80 system/manager @d:\chris\sql\generate_back.sql
plus80 system/manager @d:\chris\sql\runback.sql
```

GENERATE_BACK.SQL

```
set heading off
set feedback off
set termout off
set echo off
spool d:\chris\sql\runback.sql
select 'set heading off' from dual;
select 'set echo on' from dual;
select 'spool c:\backup\runback.out' from dual;
select 'select ''backup started on'',TO_CHAR(SYSDATE, ''fmMonth
DD, YYYY:HH:MI:SS'') from dual;' from dual;
select 'alter tablespace '||tablespace_name||' begin backup;'
from sys.dba_tablespaces;
select ' host ocopy80 '||file_name||' c:\backup' from
sys.dba_data_files;
select 'alter tablespace '||tablespace_name||' end backup;' from
sys.dba_tablespaces;
select 'alter system switch logfile;' from dual;
select 'alter database backup controlfile to
''c:\backup\cntrlfile.bck'' reuse;' from dual;
select 'alter database backup controlfile to trace;' from dual;
select 'select ''backup ended on'',TO_CHAR(SYSDATE, ''fmMonth
DD, YYYY:HH:MI:SS'') from dual;' from dual;
select 'spool off' from dual;
select 'exit' from dual;
spool off
exit
```

Hot Backup Scripts for UNIX

This script is a little different. It runs on UNIX, does some simple error checking and backs up the tablespace datafiles one at a time so it won't dominate the I/O channels. Once again, use at your own risk. It works great for us. A junior DBA that is quickly surpassing me in many areas wrote this script (darn kids).

The first script calls the second and passes two variables. *unixbackup.ksh* sets several variables that will be used throughout the two scripts. Runtime messages are written to *hotbackup.log*. *unixbackup.ksh* calls *generate_hotbackup.ksh* which reads the data dictionary and writes the backup commands to *runhotback.sql*. *unixbackup.ksh* then performs the actual backup by running *runhotback.sql*.

💾 UNIXBACKUP.KSH

```
#!/bin/ksh
ORACLE_SID=cif
export ORACLE_SID
GEN_BACKUP=/home/oracle/cif/scripts/generate_hotbackup.ksh
export GEN_BACKUP
RUN_BACKUP=/home/oracle/cif/tmp/runhotback.sql
export RUN_BACKUP
BACKUP_LOG=/home/oracle/cif/logs/hotbackup.log
export BACKUP_LOG
ARCH_DEST=/orcarc/cif
export ARCH_DEST
BACKUP_ARCH=
export BACKUP_ARCH
HOTBACKUP=/orc10/cif/backup
export HOTBACKUP
PROG=`basename $0`;export PROG
echo "Starting the Database Hot Backup" > $BACKUP_LOG

if
[ ! -f $GEN_BACKUP ]
then
    echo "Shell Script $GEN_BACKUP not found!" >> $BACKUP_LOG
    exit 1
```

```
if
$GEN_BACKUP $HOTBACKUP $RUN_BACKUP

if
[ $? -ne 0 ]

then
echo "execution of $GEN_BACKUP failed." >> $BACKUP_LOG
exit 1
if

echo "
@$RUN_BACKUP
" | sqlplus / >> $BACKUP_LOG
if
[ $? -ne 0 ]

then
echo "execution of $RUN_BACKUP failed." >> $BACKUP_LOG
exit 1

if

egrep "DBA-|ORA-" $BACKUP_LOG > /dev/null
if [ $? -eq 0 ]

then
echo "errors were detected while performing a hot backup." >>
$BACKUP_LOG
echo "hot backup failed." >> $BACKUP_LOG
else
echo "hot backup completed successfully." >> $BACKUP_LOG
if
exit 0
```

💾 GENERATE_HOTBACKUP.KSH

```
#!/bin/ksh
HOT_BACKUP=$1
RUN_BACKUP=$2
OUT_BACKUP=${RUN_BACKUP%.*}.out
sqlplus -s / << eof
set heading off
set feedback off
set termout off
set echo off
spool $RUN_BACKUP
select 'set heading off' from dual;
select 'set echo on' from dual;
select 'alter session set NLS_DATE_FORMAT = ''DD-MON-YY,
HH24:MI:SS'';' from dual;
select 'spool $OUT_BACKUP;' from dual;
select 'select ''backup started on:'',SYSDATE from dual;' from
dual;
select 'alter system switch logfile;' from dual;
select 'alter tablespace '||tablespace_name||' begin backup;'
from sys.dba_tablespaces;
```

```
select ''||tablespace_name||' ! cp '||file_name||' $HOT_BACKUP'
from sys.dba_data_files;
select 'alter tablespace '||tablespace_name||' end backup;' from
sys.dba_tablespaces;
select 'alter system switch logfile;' from dual;
select 'alter database backup controlfile to
''$HOT_BACKUP/cntrlfile.bck'' reuse;' from dual;
select 'alter database backup controlfile to trace;' from dual;
select 'select ''backup ended on:'',SYSDATE from dual;' from
dual;
select 'spool off' from dual;
select 'exit' from dual;
spool off
exit
eof
nawk '{if(($3 == "cp") && ($5 == backdest))
{
split($4,fname,"/");
printf("%s%s%s\n %s%s %s %s\n %s%s/%s\n%s%s%s\n", "alter
tablespace ", $1, " begin backup;", $2, $3, $4, $5, "!compress
", backdest, fname[5], "alter tablespace ", $1, " end backup;")
}
else {print $0}}' < $RUN_BACKUP backdest=$HOT_BACKUP > tmpfile

/usr/bin/mv tmpfile $RUN_BACKUP
```

Oracle9i – Lazy Checkpointer

In previous releases of Oracle, a total system checkpoint occurred during log switches. A total system checkpoint flushes all of the changes recorded in the redo log that was just filled to the datafiles. If the recently filled logfile ended up missing or became corrupt, the administrator could easily correct the situation by issuing the 'ALTER SYSTEM CLEAR LOGFILE XXX;' command. If the file were missing, it would be recreated and if it were corrupt it would be reinitialized. This statement overcomes two situations where dropping redo logs is not possible: there are only two log groups or the corrupt redo log file belongs to the current group. If there are more than two redo log groups and the corrupt redo log file does NOT belong to the current group, the DBA also has the option of dropping and recreating the corrupt redo log group.

Oracle9i performs lazy checkpoints during a log switch. As a result, all of the changes recorded by the recently filled redo log may not be flushed to the datafiles. When the administrator tries to execute the 'ALTER SYSTEM CLEAR LOGFILE XXX;' command the dreaded 'LOGFILE NEEDED FOR TRANSACTION RECOVERY' may be returned.

The above error message was returned because the lazy checkpoint did not flush the changes recorded in the recently filled redo log to the datafiles. Before executing other recover strategies (or printing off resumes and cover pages), administrators should execute the 'ALTER SYSTEM CHECKPOINT' command. This will force the system to flush the changes to the datafiles. The administrator should then reexecute the 'ALTER SYSTEM CLEAR LOGFILE XXX;' command.

If that doesn't work, the database cannot be made consistent and the administrator is now forced to bring all of the datafiles from the last backup and perform a CANCEL based recovery. The administrator would type in CANCEL when prompted for the missing online redo log.

All of the Oracle certification tests will have numerous questions on checkpoint processing. Test candidates should have a very strong and thorough knowledge of Oracle checkpoints including:

- What activates checkpoints
- The processing that occurs during a checkpoint
- The difference between a checkpoint and a commit

- The database objects that are impacted by checkpoints
    - Online redo log files
    - Control files
    - Data files
- Fast start on-demand rollback
- Initialization parameters influencing checkpoints
    - *fast_start_mttr_target*
    - *log_checkpoint_timeout*
    - *log_checkpoint_interval*
- Understand how to use *v$instance_recovery* to estimate instance recovery times
- The impact checkpointing has on Oracle performance

Recovery Manager

Whether you love it or hate it, the Oracle Recovery Manager (RMAN) tool is here to stay. Sometime in your career, you will have to deal with it. Here's my two-cents. It seems to complicate the backup process and simplify the recovery process.

Recovery Manager allows administrators to write scripts, test and store them in the recovery catalog. The tool really does simplify the recovery process. The administrator picks the script and runs it - recovery complete! Running a script or two at 2AM is usually preferable to sitting at your PC trying to paste together a recovery procedure. Here is some general information on the Recovery Manager toolset.

Recovery Manager is a utility that you can use to create backups and recover database files. The work of creating and restoring from backup files is done inside the Oracle server. Recovery Manager uses a special program interface to the server for invoking backup and restore operations.

Recovery Manager provides the following benefits:
- Automates backup operations.
- Creates printable logs of all backup and recovery operations.
- Automates both restore media and recovery operations.
- Automatically parallelizes backup and recovery.
- Configures backups for later execution.
- Automatically finds datafiles that need a backup based on user-specified limits on the amount of redo that must be applied if the datafiles were to be recovered.

Notice that the key word is automate! Many of the operations that once required manual intervention by the administrator are now automated. Recovery Manager automatically starts Oracle server processes that backup and recover the target databases.

Recovery Manager can be run in either interactive or batch mode. In interactive mode, Recovery Manager will immediately execute commands as you enter them at the prompt. Batch mode allows system job control programs to run regularly scheduled backups. Both batch and interactive mode provide message logging to record significant actions taken by Recovery Manager.

Recovery Catalog

The recovery catalog can be loosely compared to a database catalog. Recovery manager uses the catalog's repository of information to keep track of backup and recovery operations. The recovery catalog must be contained in an Oracle database but does not require the creation of an additional database. The catalog can be placed in an existing database if desired. The recovery catalog contains information on:

- Tablespaces and datafiles
- Archived redo logs (and copies of archived redo logs)
- Datafile copies
- Datafile and archivelog backup sets and backup pieces
- Stored scripts which contain user created sequences of commands that can be executed by the Recovery Manager

Administrators can create scripts and store them in the recovery catalog. Stored scripts allow administrators to chain a sequence of backup or recovery operations together and execute them as a single unit.

Recovery Manager Backup Types

Recovery Manager supports two different types of backups: backup sets and image copies.

Backup Sets

Backup sets consist of datafiles or archivelogs. A single backup set cannot contain a combination of archivelogs and datafiles. A backup set can contain a combination of datafile and control file backups. Recovery Manager allows you to move archived logs from disk to tape. Backup sets containing moved archived logs are called archivelog backup sets.

Backup sets consist of one or more individual backup files. The individual files contained in a backup set are called backup pieces. Recovery Manager uses the backup sets as input for recovery operations. Backup sets can be written to disk or sequential output media. The *v$backup_device* contains a list of backup devices that are supported by your platform.

Backup sets can be full or incremental. A full backup is a backup of all of the blocks that make up a datafile or datafiles. Recovery Manager allows you to take full backups of datafiles, datafile copies, tablespaces, archive logs, control files and databases. Incremental backups copy blocks that have been changed since a previous backup. Incremental copes can be taken of datafiles, tablespaces and databases. Recovery Manager also provides cumulative backups. Cumulative backups copy all blocks that have been changed since the most recent incremental backup.

Image Copies

An image copy is a single datafile that is produced by an Oracle server process that you can use as input to a recovery. The Oracle server process validates the blocks in the file during backup and registers the copy in the recovery catalog. Image copies do not require the execution of a recovery operation, the datafile can be renamed to the image copy. As a result, image copies:

- Do not store header or footer control information.
- Must be written to disk.
- Cannot be compressed.
- Cannot contain multiple input or output files.
- Cannot be multiplexed (discussed later).

Parallel Backup and Recovery

Recovery Manager is able to parallelize a single backup, recovery or restore operation, but is unable to process multiple commands in a stored script in parallel.

Multiplexed Backup Sets

A backup process is able to take concurrent backups of multiple data files, or one or more multi-file tablespaces and multiplex the output into a single stream.

Backup/Recovery Reports

Recovery Manager provides two commands to provide information relating to backups and image copies:

- Report - produces a report of files that require backups, files that are unrecoverable and backup files that can be deleted.

- List - produces a listing of the contents of the recovery catalog. The list command allows you to find out what backups or copies are available.

Database Recovery

You use the RECOVER command in Recovery Manager to perform media recovery and apply incremental backups. Recovery Manager uses the recovery catalog to select the backup sets or image copies to use as input to the recovery operation. If the recovery catalog is unavailable, Recovery Manager will use the database's control file to perform the recovery.

There are three variations of the recover command:

- RECOVER DATABASE - recovers an entire database.
- RECOVER TABLESPACE - recovers an entire tablespace consisting of one or more datafiles.
- RECOVER DATAFILE - recovers a single datafile or datafiles.

RMAN Examples

The examples below should give you a general understanding of how RMAN is used to back up and recover an Oracle database:

- rman - Operating system command to activate RMAN. There is also a GUI version available in later releases.
- CONNECT TARGET SYS/sysdba@prod1 - Connecting to the target database (the one that is to be backed up or recovered).

- CONNECT CATALOG rman/rman@rcat - Connecting to the database containing the RMAN catalog.

- rman TARGET SYS/target_pwd@target_str CATALOG rman/cat_pwd@cat_str - Getting high-tech and connecting to both the target and RMAN catalog at the same time.

- CREATE CATALOG; - Creating the catalog in the RMAN repository database.

- REPORT SCHEMA; - Displays the datafiles currently in the target database.

- LIST BACKUP SUMMARY; - Displays a summary of all backups recorded in the catalog.

- LIST COPY OF DATABASE ARCHIVELOG ALL; - Lists archived logs and copies of logs.

This command uses two backupSpec clauses to back up tablespaces and datafiles and lets RMAN perform automatic parallelization of the backup. A channel must be allocated when it accesses a disk or tape drive. The backup is identifying files by tablespace name and fileid.

```
RUN
{
  ALLOCATE CHANNEL dev1 DEVICE TYPE DISK FORMAT '/fs1/%U';
  ALLOCATE CHANNEL dev2 DEVICE TYPE DISK FORMAT '/fs2/%U';
  BACKUP
    (TABLESPACE SYSTEM,sales1,sales2,sales3 FILESPERSET 20)
    (DATAFILE 12,14,15);
}
```

This next example uses the preconfigured disk channel and manually allocates one media management channel to use datafile copies on disk and backups on tape, and restores one of the datafiles in tablespace tbs_1 to a different location:

```
RUN
{
  ALLOCATE CHANNEL dev1 DEVICE TYPE DISK FORMAT '/fs1/%U';
  ALLOCATE CHANNEL dev2 DEVICE TYPE DISK FORMAT '/fs2/%U';
  BACKUP
    (TABLESPACE SYSTEM,sales1,sales2,sales3 FILESPERSET 20)
    (DATAFILE 12,14,15);
}
```

The Oracle Database Fundamentals II (1Z0-032) certification test will have numerous questions on the Oracle Recovery Manager Utility. Test candidates must have a thorough knowledge of RMAN to pass the test. The information the test is covered pretty thoroughly in the Oracle Certification Test Preparation chapter. Rest assured that at least 30% to 40% of the questions in the test will be on the Oracle Recovery Manager Utility. If you don't know RMAN, you will not pass the test.

db_verify

db_verify is an Oracle supplied command line utility that can be used to verify the contents of database datafiles or backups of database datafiles. *db_verify* allows administrators to verify that the contents of a backup file are complete and correct before applying the file in a restore operation. *db_verify* can also be used to verify the contents of a database datafile when data corruption is a possibility.

Conclusion

Recovering an Oracle database is not really as complex as it seems. This chapter provided a few helpful hints and tips to make your next restoration easier, and hopefully, less stressful. A few quick points to remember from this chapter are:

- Successful recoveries depend upon good backups. I have never seen the database make a mistake during the recovery process. That leaves incomplete backups and DBA error as the most likely causes of "recoveries gone bad."

- RELAX and plan your attack. Do not begin pasting the database back together without a plan. Write it down and have someone review it. A second opinion may prevent you from making a mistake or overlooking a key part of the recovery process.

- Read the Oracle Backup and Recovery before reading third-party books. The manuals will provide you with a firm foundation of knowledge on backup and recovery strategies and procedures. Then move on to third-party books (like this one) for helpful hints and tips that may assist you in the recovery process.

- Take the backup and recovery class!

- Keep your recovery skills sharp by performing test recoveries on a regular basis. We have a test machine in our labs at Contemporary Technologies. On a regular basis, one of our senior-level DBAs will destroy the test database and the next DBA up on the "test recovery list" has to recover the database. It has actually become quite an interesting game over the years with bragging rights over who has the title of "the most devious database destroyer." The more test recoveries you do the easier the production recoveries become.

- New highly-available architectures (redundant disks, striping, etc.) have a tendency to make DBAs complacent. Do not rely upon advanced architectures to keep your database safe. Learn the basics of backup and recovery and be ready to use them when required.

Now that we have covered backup and recovery, the next logical topic is tuning and performance.

Tuning and Performance

CHAPTER 7

One of the great benefits of Oracle is that it has an abundance of tuning "knobs" that a DBA can use to increase performance. One of the great drawbacks of Oracle is that it has an abundance of tuning "knobs" that a DBA can use to increase performance. Tuning Oracle can be challenging. The key to being a good tuner is to become as educated as you can about Oracle tuning parameters, the tuning process and the tools used to collect tuning information. Good tuners understand that the tuning process starts with an understanding of the problem then continues with the DBA collecting statistical information. Information collection begins at a global level and then narrows in scope until the problem is pinpointed.

Be careful with the ANALYZE command

The ANALYZE command collects statistical information about data for the cost-based optimizer. The cost-based optimizer uses this information to determine the optimal access path to the data. Running ANALYZE on a regular basis is the key to good query performance (the more current the statistics the better). But, there is a potential problem for those that have their *optimizer_mode* set to CHOOSE.

If *optimizer_mode* is set to CHOOSE, the optimizer is able to switch between rule and cost-based optimizations.

When set to CHOOSE, the optimizer uses the cost-based approach for a SQL statement if there are statistics in the dictionary for at least one table accessed in the statement. If you run ANALYZE on one table, every query that accesses that table will use the cost-based optimizer. What happens if other tables in the query did not have ANALYZE run and, as a result, do not have statistics collected? The optimizer will make an educated guess. The problem is that Oracle isn't always a good statistics "guesser" and the end-result is a "less than optimal" access path.

The Oracle Database Performance Tuning (1Z0-033) certification test will have a few questions on the analyze command. Test candidates should know:

- The specifications used to execute the analyze command including histograms

- The impact running analyze has on the Oracle cost based optimizer

- Exporting and importing data object statistics

Finding Problem Queries

Execute the following query to identify the SQL responsible for the most disk reads:

```
SELECT disk_reads, executions, disk_reads/executions, sql_text
FROM v$sqlarea WHERE disk_reads > 5000 ORDER BY disk_reads;
```

Execute the following query to identify the SQL responsible for the most buffer hits:

```
SELECT buffer_gets, executions, buffer_gets/executions, sql_text
FROM v$sqlarea WHERE buffer_gets > 100000 ORDER BY buffer_gets;
```

When I was first starting as a DBA, an Oracle consultant was kind enough to send me an entire directory's worth of tuning scripts. These two queries were contained in the directory along with a couple of dozen others that provided buffer hit ratios and other performance related statistical information. I never knew that that these two queries were the most important ones in the bunch. That was until I attended an IOUG presentation given by Richard Niemiec from TUSC. Rich focused on the benefits that these two queries provide, the light bulb finally came on (thanks Rich) and I now use them religiously.

It's common knowledge that poorly performing SQL is responsible for the majority of database performance problems. The first query returns SQL statements responsible for generating disk reads greater than 5,000 while the second query returns SQL statements responsible for generating buffer reads greater than 100,000. These are good numbers to start with and you can adjust them according to the size of the system you are tuning. I modified the original queries to divide the number of disk and buffer reads by the number of statement executions. If a statement is generating 1,000,000 disk reads but is executed 500,000 times, it probably doesn't need tuning.

Heavy disk reads per statement execution usually means a lack of proper indexing. Heavy buffer reads usually means the exact opposite - indexes are being used when they shouldn't be. Further information on how to tune heavy resource consuming queries is beyond the scope of this article.

Optimizer Plan Stability

Oracle8i provided administrators with the capability to "freeze" access paths and store them in the database. The access path to the data remains constant despite data changes, data object changes and upgrades of the database or application software. Administrators are able to determine which statements use the frozen access paths and which statements will have their access paths determined during statement execution.

Optimizer plan stability provides predictable application performance, which offers great benefits to third-party vendors that distribute packaged applications. Third-party application vendors are now able to ensure that the same access paths are being used regardless of the environment their applications are running in.

Optimizer plan stability also benefits online transaction processing (OLTP) applications by allowing SQL statements to execute without having to call the optimizer to create an access path. This allows complex SQL to be executed without the additional overhead required by the optimizer to perform the calculations necessary to determine the most efficient access path to the data.

Optimizer plan stability stores predefined execution plans in a stored outline. You can create a stored outline for one or more SQL statements. The optimizer is able to generate an execution plan by using the information in the stored outline. Oracle also allows administrators to choose from multiple outlines (and multiple access paths). The SQL statement being executed must exactly match the text stored in an outline for it to use the predefined execution plan. Oracle considers any SQL text differences a mismatch and will not use the stored outline.

The *use_stored_outlines* parameter is set to TRUE or to a category name to enable the use of stored outlines. If you set *use_stored_outlines* to TRUE, Oracle will use the access paths owned by the DEFAULT outline category. If you specify a category name with the *use_stored_outlines* parameter, Oracle uses outlines in that category. If you specify a category name and Oracle does not find an outline in that category that matches the SQL statement, Oracle searches for an outline in the DEFAULT category.

The Oracle Database Performance Tuning (1Z0-033) certification test will also contain a few questions on the Oracle9i Optimizer Plan Stability Feature. Test candidates should have an understanding of:

- A basic understanding of Optimizer Plan Stability and the benefits it provides
- How to activate, configure and administer Optimizer Plan Stability

Pinning Objects in the Shared Pool

Loading the same objects into the shared pool repeatedly and shared pool fragmentation are common problems in many Oracle databases. The keys to tuning the shared pool are:

- Identifying the objects being reloaded into the shared pool time and time again:

```
SELECT owner, name||' - '||type name, loads , sharable_mem
FROM v$db_object_cache WHERE loads > 1 AND type IN
('PACKAGE', 'PACKAGE BODY', 'FUNCTION', 'PROCEDURE') ORDER
BY loads DESC;
```

- Identifying large objects that may not be able to be loaded into a fragmented shared pool:

```
SELECT owner, name||' - '||type name, sharable_mem FROM
v$db_object_cache WHERE sharable_mem > 10000 AND type IN
('PACKAGE', 'PACKAGE BODY', 'FUNCTION', 'PROCEDURE')ORDER BY
sharable_mem DESC;
```

The objects identified by the above queries can be pinned in the shared pool by executing the *dbms_shared_pool.keep* procedure. Several Oracle supplied packages that should be pinned in the shared pool are STANDARD, DBMS_STANDARD and UTIL. The objects must be pinned every time the Oracle database is started.

PCTFREE and PCTUSED

If you don't have enough information to make an educated guess on these parameters, don't make an uneducated one. Select the default values and monitor for chained rows by using the LIST CHAINED ROWS option in the ANALYZE statement.

Caching Tables

If you have small lookup (some call them code or domain) tables that are being forced out of memory, you can attempt to persuade Oracle to allow them to stay longer in memory by specifying the CACHE parameter of the CREATE and ALTER database statements. You can also use the CACHE hint on SQL statements to toggle caching on and off. A common misconception is that the CACHE option forces tables into memory and they are never aged out. When Oracle reads blocks accessed with a full table scan, it moves the blocks' addresses to the LRU side of the Least Recently Used (LRU) list. The intent is to flush the blocks read by a table scan out of the cache more quickly than blocks read by direct reads. The problem is that smaller tables, like lookup tables, are most often scanned by a full table scan (and they should be). The CACHE parameter forces Oracle to place the results on the Most Recently Used side of the LRU list. They will still age out, only not as quickly.

Clustering Data in Tables

Before clusters, Oracle didn't have a mechanism to sort data in a table to match the order of a particular index. But clusters can be difficult to tune and administer, yet they do increase performance in certain (limited) circumstances. If you can't (or don't want to) use clusters, try this option. If the application always accesses the table by the same column or the table is always joined to other tables by the same column, consider sorting the data on that column before loading. Static tables are the easiest to sort, but I have seen administrators in OLTP systems pump data out of tables into flat files, sort the records in the proper order and reload them using the load utility on a regular basis.

Merging Tables to Increase Query Performance

If you constantly join two or more tables together in an application, merge them into one table. It's called "de-normalizing for performance" (your data administrator make call it and you other things). It's simple and it works.

Hints

Don't use hints unless it is absolutely necessary. You are altering SQL to influence the optimizer. This may have a negative impact when the data, application or database release changes. Application performance may be negatively impacted when any of the aforementioned changes occur and you won't know why. It's a safe assumption that, in most cases, we aren't as smart as the optimizer. Let it make the choice unless you are certain the optimizer is choosing the incorrect access path. One exception to the rule is when you use Oracle's Parallel Query Option (see next recommendation). Remember a hint in Oracle is just that – a hint. You can't force the optimizer to choose an access path. That's why they call it a hint!

The Oracle Database Performance Tuning (1Z0-033) certification test will have a few questions on SQL hints. Test candidates should understand:

- Basic hint syntax
- The effect hints have on the Oracle cost based optimizer
- A few of the more commonly used hints
    - o Table scan hints
    - o Index hints
    - o Join order hints

- Join hints
    - Nested loop
    - Merge scan
    - Hybrid
- Optimizer hints
    - First rows
    - All rows
    - Rule

Parallel Hints

Oracle allows you to set the degree of parallelism for queries at the database, table and statement levels. Statement hints allow you to fine tune individual statements without increasing or decreasing the degree of parallelism for other statements. Set the degree of parallelism at the database and table level carefully.

Performance Testing

The buffer cache can magically increase the performance of SQL benchmarking tests. The first run will incur the I/O to load the data buffers and subsequent runs may be faster because the data is now cached.

Parallel Query

Use profiles in a pre-Oracle8i parallel query environment to limit the number of simultaneous sessions to the database to "throttle" the number of parallel query processes spawned. When using parallel query, users ca get a lot of multiple processes even with a fairly low parallel degree on the tables. A two table join with both tables having DEGREE=4 would use 9 sessions (4 per table + 1 for SQL*Plus). With a hundred users, this adds up quickly. If a user's profile limits the number of user sessions allowed, Oracle will parallelize one table and single thread through the other.

Tuning Oracle on Windows

There are two quick changes you can make on Windows platforms to improve performance.

- Change the machine configuration from the default "Maximize throughput for file sharing" to "Maximize throughput for network applications" (Right click on Network Neighborhood/ Services/ Server/ Properties).

- Make sure that all threads run with NORMAL priority (see *oracle_priority* registry value).

Tuning Pack

In my very unscientific polling of numerous DBAs, the Oracle Tuning Pack was rated to be the most beneficial of the three packs that Oracle provides. The Expert Advisor is intelligent. If you don't have tuning expertise, you can use it to overcome your lack of experience.

Direct Load Inserts

Oracle8 increased the performance of SQL INSERT statements by providing a direct load INSERT statement. The direct load INSERT, also known as INSERT APPEND, bypasses the database buffer cache and inserts data rows directly into the datafiles (much like the direct load utility).

Direct load INSERTs are able to access both partitioned and non-partitioned tables and are able to be executed in parallel. In addition, administrators are able to turn logging off to increase performance of the direct load INSERT statement. The ALTER TABLE, ALTER INDEX or ALTER TABLESPACE command is used to activate logging/nologging on the target objects. A COMMIT or ROLLBACK statement is required to be executed immediately after the completion of the direct load insert.

Direct load INSERTs use more space than conventional path INSERTs because they append data beyond the high water mark. Conventional path INSERTs are able to reuse freespace below the high water mark. Direct load INSERTs can not be used if there are any global indexes or referential constraints on the table.

Only the INSERT...SELECT syntax can process direct load inserts in parallel. The INSERT.....values variation of the insert statement can not execute in parallel. You activate direct load INSERTs by specifing a hint in the INSERT statement. The following examples show how to use hints to activate direct load INSERTs:

```
INSERT /*+ APPEND */ INTO us_employees VALUES .....;
```

Uses direct load INSERT to insert a list of values into the us_employees table.

```
INSERT /*+ PARALLEL (us_employees, 4) */ INTO us_employees
SELECT /*+ PARALLEL (total_employees, 4) */ FROM
total_employees;
```

Uses direct load insert with the parallel option. We are using several parallel hints in this statement to parallelize both the INSERT and SELECT operations. The APPEND hint is not required, since it is implied by the PARALLEL hint.

Parallel DML Processing

Oracle Version 7 allowed users to parallelize SQL SELECT statements to increase application performance. Parallelism increases query performance by splitting the work among multiple child processes.

Oracle8 enhanced Oracle's parallel feature by allowing administrators to parallelize INSERT, UPDATE and DELETE statements. Parallel DML is particularly useful for decision support applications that contain large amounts of data.

In releases previous to Oracle9i Release 2, UPDATE and DELETE statements could only be parallelized on partitioned tables. They could not access individual partitions or non-partitioned tables in parallel. A parallel UPDATE/DELETE process is able to access multiple partitions during its execution but a single partition can only be updated or deleted by a single parallel process.

In Oracle9i Release 2, parallel DML child processes can access non-partitioned tables. Please refer to the Oracle9i Release 2 Data Warehousing Guide for more information on enabling parallel DML statements.

Unlike UPDATE and DELETE statements, INSERT statements can be parallelized on both non-partitioned and partitioned tables in all Oracle releases that support parallel DML. Remember, only direct load INSERT...SELECT statements can process in parallel. The INSERT.....values variation of the INSERT statement and conventional INSERTs can not execute in parallel.

You enable parallel DML processing by using the ALTER SESSION ENABLE PARALLEL DML statement. The Oracle manual states that this is necessary because parallel DML has different locking, transaction and disk space requirements than non-parallel DML.

After the ALTER SESSION ENABLE PARALLEL DML statement is executed, Oracle will consider the next DML statement for parallel execution. This mode does not have an affect on any queries in the transaction that may be executed in parallel. Altering the session to enable DML parallelism does not always guarantee the DML statement will be executed in parallel. You activate DML parallelism by:

- Setting the PARALLEL specification on a table or index to specify the default degree of parallelism for that particular object.

- Coding a hint in the DML statement that is to be executed in parallel.

In addition to the requirements listed above, the following restrictions apply to direct load INSERTs and parallel DML:

Parallel DML Processing **197**

- A parallel DML statement must be the first and only DML statement in a transaction. The work must be explicitly committed or rolled back after the execution of the parallel DML statement.

- Parallel UPDATE and DELETE processes cannot execute on a single partition (see above).

- Parallel DML does not fire triggers. As a result, Oracle replication does not support parallel DML.

- Parallel DML cannot execute against tables containing self-referencing referential integrity constraints, DELETE CASCADE option and deferrable integrity constraints.

Materialized Views

In releases previous to Oracle8i, administrators used summary tables to increase SQL performance for data warehousing applications. A summary table stores the pre-computed results of data calculations, such as sums, counts, averages and data table joins. It is more efficient to access a pre-computed result instead of computing the desired result from detail data every time a query is executed. In Oracle8i and later releases, administrators are able to use materialized views to provide the same benefits as summary tables.

An example that Oracle often uses in its materialized view demos is the sales-per-region-per-month materialized views. When a SQL statement is executed that calculates all sales for the Eastern region for the first quarter, the Oracle database will not calculate the total sales from individual sales detail records. Oracle will use the query-rewrite feature to rewrite the query to retrieve the summarized data from the sales-per-region-per-month materialized view. Because the optimizer automatically rewrites the query to use the summarized data, the use of the materialized view is entirely transparent to the end-user. No SQL or application changes required.

Oracle reference manuals provide a wealth of information on materialized views. This feature has become very popular with data warehouse developers and database administrators. Why should queries be forced to read every detail row when they are looking for summarized information?

The Oracle Database Performance Tuning (1Z0-033) certification test may have a question or two on materialized views. Test candidates should know:

- The basics of materialized views and the effect they have on query performance
- How to create and modify materialized views
- The various ways to refresh materialized views
- Query rewrite
- The DBMS_MVIEW package

Database Resource Management

Managing CPU, memory and disk resources for Oracle database servers is challenging (to say the least). In previous releases, Oracle was unable to determine a transaction's priority. The result was that critical transactions were given the same amount of resources as their less critical counterparts. Oracle8i corrected this deficiency by introducing resource management, which provides the administrator with greater control of system resources assigned to users and groups of users.

It is now possible to allocate system resources among tasks of varying importance to achieve overall performance goals. Important online users, such as transaction entry operators can be given a higher priority than users running batch reports. Users are assigned to resource classes, such as "CLERK", "DECISION_SUPPORT", "BATCH" or "DEVELOPER." Each resource class is allocated a portion of system resources. High priority classes can be given more resources than lower priority classes. In addition, the degree of parallelism of any operation can also be limited.

Oracle continues to enhance database resource management with every new release. Oracle9i provides administrators with a GUI screen that can be used to administer a DRM environment. The Oracle New Features guide provides a listing of all of the other enhancements related to DRM.

STATSPACK

Oracle database administrators have been using UTLBSTAT/UTLESTAT (affectionately known as BSTAT/ESTAT) to solve performance problems for some time now (actually a very long time now). A few of the well-known limitations of BSTAT/ESTAT are:

- Since the data is deleted by ESTAT after the reports are run, administrators were unable to provide a historical view of performance data.

- The reporting capabilities were very limited and the output was disorganized and hard to understand.
- The reports did not contain the full set of statistics required to effectively tune the database.
- The reports did not provide a listing of poorly performing SQL statements which are a contributor to poor database performance.
- BSTAT/ESTAT does not take all of the new "bells and whistles" contained in each new Oracle release into consideration.

Oracle version 8.1.6 addressed some of these deficiencies with STATSPACK. STATSPACK provides the following features:

- A much larger set of performance statistics are collected and reported on.
- A report listing of high resource consuming SQL statements is now provided.
- Many of the manual calculations required by ESTAT/ESTAT to measure database performance are automated.
- STATSPACK creates permanent performance data tables, which are used to contain output from the snapshots. As a result, administrators can compare the output from multiple STATSPACK executions and review the data at any time.
- Since STATSPACK is a PL/SQL package, it can be executed by CRON, AT or DBMSJOB.
- A snapshot ID is used to identify the reporting data and can be used to easily compare the output generated by the different SNAPSHOT executions.

- Oracle provides the PERFSTAT account that is created when STATSPACK is installed. All performance data tables and programs are owned by PERFSTAT.
- SQL*Plus can be used to both execute the snapshots and create the reports.

Like *utlbstat.sql* and *utlestat.sql*, STATSPACK can be found in the ORACLE_HOME/rdbms/admin/ directory on UNIX and in the ORACLE_HOME/rdbms81/admin directory on Windows servers.

V$ TABLES vs. Oracle BSTAT/ESTAT and STATSPACK

Remember that many V$ tables are cumulative in nature. They track information since the database has been started. The information collected by BSTAT/ESTAT and STATSPACK are "snapshots" of information captured during the tool's execution. If you are interested in seeing how the database is performing during a specific time-period, don't use the V$ tables since they are cumulative. Pick the time period that you want to run statistics and run STATSPACK instead.

Segment-Level Performance Statistics Collection

Starting with Oracle9i Release 2, administrators are able to gather statistics at the individual segment level. Don't confuse segment-level performance statistics with optimizer statistics generated from a *dbms_stats* execution or SQL ANALYZE statement.

Segment-level performance statistics are a subset of the statistics captured at the system level. A list of the statistics captured is as follows:

- Logicial reads – buffers used for consistent and current reads
- Buffer busy waits – waits caused by a buffer that is in use
- Db block changes – changes applied to buffers
- Physical reads – number of physical reads
- Physical writes – number of physical writes
- Physical reads direct – number of direct reads
- Physical writes direct – number of direct writes
- ITL waits – waits caused by no ITL entry
- Row lock waits – waits caused by row lock contention
- Global cache cr blocks served – Real Application Cluster statistical information
- Global cache current blocks served – Real Application Cluster statistical information

When investigating performance problems, administrators would use the system-wide statistics contained in the V$ views to review performance indicators at the instance level. Segment-level performance statistics can then be used to focus on the specific tables and indexes that may be causing the problem.

Segment-Level Performance Statistics Collection   **203**

Statistics are captured by setting the *statistics_level* dynamic initialization parameter to TRUE (default) or ALL. Although a small section of the SGA is allocated to capture this information, there is no significant impact on database performance.

Three new dynamic performance views are introduced in Oracle 9i Release 2:

- *v$segstat_name* – lists the segment statistics collected
- *v$segstat* – real time monitoring view of segment-level statistics
- *v$segment_statistics* – contains all of the information in *v$segstat* plus segment owner, tablespace name, etc.

Performance Tuning Intelligent Advisories

Experienced DBAs often start their tuning efforts by selecting data from the V$ dynamic performance tables to view system-wide performance indicators. For those of you new to Oracle, statistics are pieces of information that the Oracle instance collects to help administrators gauge performance and identify problems. But intelligent performance advisories are a relatively new concept (they are introduced in Oracle9i), so a quick definition is in order before we continue.

An advisory is a collection of information that predicts the impact a specific change would have on the item being monitored. Advisories allow administrators to simulate "what if" hypothetical scenarios to predict the impact a specific change may have on the Oracle environment.

For example, the *v$shared_pool_advice* view contains information about estimated parse time savings if a different shared pool size were used. Each row in the view contains a percentage value (ranging from 50 percent to 200 percent of the current shared pool) and the estimated performance increase or decrease associated with that percentage of change.

Oracle provides advisories for the buffer cache, MTTR (Mean Time To Recovery) and PGA target. It is important to note that setting the *statistics_level* parameter alone does not activate all of the advisories. The Oracle9i Performance Tuning Guide and Reference provides information on activating and using advisories.

The Oracle Database Performance Tuning (1Z0-033) certification test will have a few questions on the new advisory feature in Oracle9i. Test candidates should have a firm understanding of:

- The different advisories that are available in Oracle9i
    - Shared pool
    - Buffer pool
    - Undo segments
- How to activate the advisories including the use of the *statistics_level* parameter

Optimizer Dynamic Sampling

So little is known about the inner-workings of the cost based optimizer that is often called the Oracle database's "little black box." The optimizer's job is to analyze the statement being executed and determine the most efficient access path to the data for that statement. Craig Mullins provides an excellent description of a database optimizer in *The DB2 Developer's Guide* "the optimizer is equivalent to an expert system. An expert system is a standard set of rules when combined with situational data can return an expert opinion."

The cost based optimizer uses statistics generated by the *dbms_stats* procedure or the ANALYZE statement as the situational data when creating its expert opinion on which access path to the data is most optimal. These statistics are stored in the data dictionary and describe the objects space characteristics, data uniqueness and data distribution.

The cost-based optimizer is only as good as the statistics it uses as input. Statistics collections should be run on a regular basis to ensure that the statistics are current (representative of the data being accessed). The optimizer is then able to create a highly accurate access path that is based on the least cost. If statistics are not available, the optimizer uses a simple algorithm to calculate the statistics, which often leads to "less than optimal" access paths. In other words, Oracle guesses and it is usually not a very good guesser.

Oracle 9i Release 2 introduces optimizer dynamic sampling to overcome the lack of accurate statistics on the objects being accessed. The optimizer is now able to take a sampling of the data during access path optimization. Administrators are able to activate dynamic sampling and control the size of the dynamic sample taken by using the *optimizer_dynamic_sampling* dynamic initialization parameter as a throttle.

The values for *optimizer_dynamic_sampling* range from 0 to 10 with 0 telling the cost-based optimizer to not use dynamic sampling and the value 10 telling the optimizer to sample all blocks in the table. The DYNAMIC SAMPLING hint can be used at the statement level to override the system setting defined by *optimizer_dynamic_sampling*.

Oracle recommends that dynamic sampling only be used when the time required to do the sample is a small fraction of the statement's total execution time. It's a safe assumption that dynamic sampling will not be used in many OLTP systems but it may find a home in a few decision support and data warehouse environments.

The Oracle Database Performance Tuning (1Z0-033) certification test may have a question on Optimizer Plan Dynamic Sampling. Test candidates should have a basic understanding of:

- The benefits that Optimizer Plan Dynamic Sampling provides
- When to use Optimizer Plan Dynamic Sampling
- How to activate Optimizer Plan Dynamic Sampling

Data Segment Compression

Compressing data has been around since the inception of the database management system. Data compression reduces the amount of data being stored, reduces memory usage (more data per memory block) and increases query performance.

Data compression in Oracle9i Release 2 is performed at the block level. Administrators are able to compress entire tables and specific table partitions. The COMPRESS attribute can be specified in the CREATE TABLE, CREATE TABLESPACE and CREATE TABLESPACE. PARTITION statements. Block compression works by eliminating repeating column values. The more repeating values the columns have the greater the compression ratio becomes.

We recently learned that compression is performed at the block level in Oracle. This means that as the number of repetitious values per block increases so does its compression ratio. Administrators are able to achieve higher compression ratios by sorting the rows on a column that has a poor cardinality (high number of repeating values). CREATE TABLE......SELECT * FROM...... ORDER BY *low_cardinality_column* can be used to ensure as many repeating values fall in the same block as possible. Flat file data being loaded by the Oracle load utility can be sorted using an operating system sort utility to achieve the same result.

Although UPDATE and DELETE operations can be performed on compressed data in Oracle, the performance impact the compress and uncompress operations have on those statements is yet to be determined. Oracle recommends that compressed data be highly considered for data warehouse environments because data block compression is highly optimized for direct-load operations.

The Oracle Database Performance Tuning (1Z0-033) certification test may have a question on Optimizer Data

Compression. Test candidates should have a basic understanding of:

- The benefits that data compression provides
- When to activate data compression

Using Explain Pan to Determine Access Paths

The "EXPLAIN PLAN" statement is used to show the access path the optimizer has chosen for a particular SQL statement.

Before issuing an EXPLAIN PLAN statement, you need to run *utlxplan.sql* to create a plan table to hold its output. *utlxplan.sql* can be found in the rdbms/admin directory in most installations. *utlxplan.sql* creates a table called *plan_table*, which is owned by the account that executed *utlxplan.sql plan_table* is the default table into which the EXPLAIN PLAN statement inserts rows describing execution plans.

You add one of the two phrases below to the beginning of the statement to notify Oracle to update the *plan_table* with rows describing the statement's access path:

- "EXPLAIN PLAN INTO schema.plan_table FOR"
- EXPLAIN PLAN INTO schema.plan_table SET STATEMENT_ID = '*******' FOR

The second statement can be used to differentiate statements in the PLAN_TABLE if it contains rows from multiple EXPLAIN PLAN statements.

The EXPLAIN PLAN specification tells the database to insert rows into the *plan_table* that describe the statement's access path. The query itself is not actually executed. The following query can be used to display the contents of the *plan_table*:

```
SELECT LPAD(' ',2*(LEVEL-1))||operation||' '||options||'
'||object_name||
' '||DECODE(id, 0, 'Cost = '||position) "Query Plan"
FROM foot.plan_table
START WITH id = 0
CONNECT BY PRIOR id = parent_id
```

The output below is an example of an EXPLAIN PLAN "dump" using the above query:

```
61844 SELECT STATEMENT      Cost = 61844
  2.1 NESTED LOOPS
    3.1 NESTED LOOPS
                4.1 TABLE ACCESS FULL PUBLISHER_REP_FIRM
                4.2 TABLE ACCESS BY ROWID APPROVAL_STATUS
                    5.1 INDEX UNIQUE SCAN
PK_APPROVAL_STATUS UNIQUE
      3.2 TABLE ACCESS BY ROWID PUBLISHER_APP
                4.1 INDEX UNIQUE SCAN PK_PUBLISHER_APP
UNIQUE
```

It is easier to understand the access path if you take the output and draw or graph the access path's steps (refer to figure 10). The statement above would produce the following graphical access path display:

```
                    2.1
                 NESTED LOOP
                /          \
           3.1              3.2
        NESTED LOOP      TABLE ACCESS
        /        \           ROWID
      4.1         4.2     PUBLISHER_APP
   TABLE ACCESS  TABLE ACCESS    |
      FULL        ROWID         4.1
 PUBLISHER_REP_FIRM APPROVAL_STATUS  INDEX UNIQUE SCAN
                      |         PK_PUBLISHER_APP
                     5.1
               INDEX UNIQUE SCAN
               PK_APPROVAL_STATUS
```

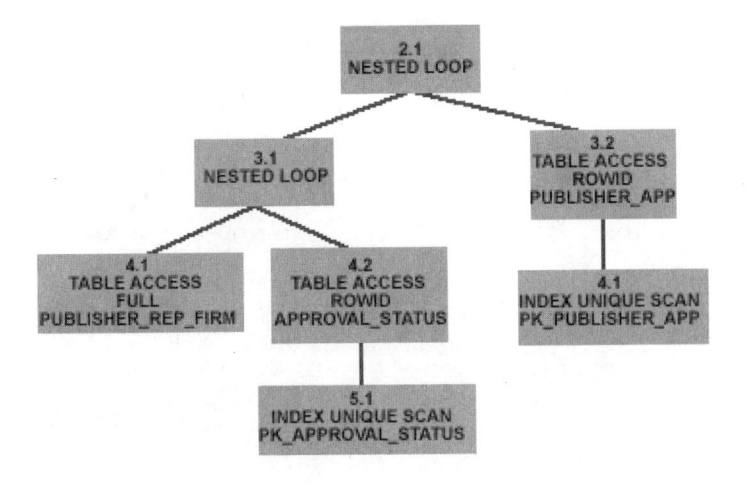

Figure 10: *Access path steps.*

Let's take a few moments to review the above access path. Although you draw the operations from the top down and left to right, Oracle will execute the operations from the left to right and then bottom to top:

- Operation 4.1 – Oracle is performing a full table scan on the outer-table PUBLISHER_REP_FIRM. Oracle must read every row in the outer-table to determine if a matching row can be found in the inner-table (APPROVAL_STATUS). You will never get the optimizer to use an index on the outer-table's join column. Oracle must read every row of the outer-table to determine if it has matching rows on the inner-table. The optimizer may choose an index on a non-join column in the outer-join table (if one is available). It's really common sense. Oracle doesn't know if there is match on the inner-table until it actually does the match! It must read every row in the outer-table to determine if there are matching values in the inner-table.

Using Explain Pan to Determine Access Paths

- Operation 5.1 – Oracle is able to use an index on the join column of the inner-table (APPROVAL_STATUS). That's because it knows the value being passed from the outer-table (PUBLISHER_REP_FIRM) during the execution of the join. It knows the value being passed to perform the match so it is able to use the unique index (PK_APPROVAL_STATUS) to get the ROWIDs of rows that match.

- Operation 4.2 – Oracle is using the ROWID retrieved in Step 5.1 to retrieve additional column values from the inner-table (APPROVAL_STATUS).

- Operation 3.1 – The nested loop join method is being used to join the two tables. The results from the join in Step 3.1 are used as the outer-table in Join 2.1. Oracle is only able to join two tables at a time. The rows are read again and the join column is used to find a match in the inner-table (PUBLISHER_APP)

- Operation 2.1 – Once again, Oracle knows the values being passed from the nested loop join (Step 3.1). Since it is being passed values to look for matching rows, it uses the index (PK_PUBLISHER_APP) which is built on the join column. Remember, the inner-table of a nested loop join can use an index on a join column (it knows the value being passed from the outer-table).

- Operation 3.2 – Oracle is using the ROWID retrieved in Step 4.1 to probe the inner-table (PK_PUBLISHER_APP).

Explain Plan Output

Because of space considerations, I am unable to cover every access path that can be selected by a particular SQL statement. In addition, the Oracle reference manuals do a pretty good (actually a very good) job of describing the various access paths a statement can take.

The Oracle8 and Oracle8i Concepts manual and the Oracle9i Database Performance Guide and Reference are the manuals to turn to when trying to learn more about Oracle access paths. The Oracle9i Database and Performance Reference Guide is the better of the three. The manual goes into great detail on what the access path actually does, factors that affect it, why the optimizer would select it and what impact it has on performance.

The Oracle Database Performance Tuning (1Z0-033) certification test will have multiple questions on Explain. Test candidates should have a firm understanding of:

- What explain tables are used for and how the simplify SQL statement tuning
- How to create an explain table
- The basic columns contained in the explain table
- How to retrieve the contents of the explain table
- How to interpret the information retrieved from the explain table

SQL*PLUS AUTOTRACE

The SQL*PLUS AUTOTRACE command can be used to create a report of the execution path used by a particular SQL statement. Statement execution statistics can also be generated if desired. This is my favorite explain tool because it's a quick and easy way to display the access path the query is taking. The following parameters are used as input to AUTOTRACE to generate different report output:

- SET AUTOTRACE OFF- No AUTOTRACE report is generated. This is the default.

- SET AUTOTRACE ON EXPLAIN - The AUTOTRACE report shows only the optimizer execution path.

- SET AUTOTRACE ON STATISTICS - The AUTOTRACE report shows only the SQL statement execution statistics.

- SET AUTOTRACE ON - The AUTOTRACE report includes both the optimizer execution path and the SQL statement execution statistics.

- SET AUTOTRACE TRACEONLY - Like SET AUTOTRACE ON, but suppresses the printing of the user's query output, if any.

High Water Mark and Table Scans

Oracle uses the high water mark to identify the highest amount of space used by a particular segment. It acts as the boundary between used and unused space. As the amount of data grows, the segment's high water mark grows accordingly. But as the amount of data shrinks (i.e. row deletes, updates), the high water mark is not altered to reflect the segment's new characteristics. The high water mark not being adjusted as the data shrinks has the tendency to create a somewhat confusing performance problem.

During a full table scan, Oracle scans all blocks up to the table's high water mark. This happens regardless of whether those blocks contain data or not. Business needs often require that all rows of a table be scanned. DBAs often attempt to increase the performance of the aforementioned table scans by trying to store as little data as possible in the scanned table. If the table is purged by SQL delete statements, the high water mark will not be moved and the table scans will continue to perform poorly.

If all of the rows are being deleted, the administrator should use the TRUNCATE statement to remove the unwanted rows. TRUNCATE adjusts the high water mark to the first block in the segment. If a partial purge is being performed, use the administrator must reorganize the table with EXPORT/IMPORT or the ALTER TABLE MOVE command.

Allocating too Much Memory to the Shared Pool and Data Buffers

Maintaining high shared pool and data buffer hit ratios is crucial for good database performance. Common recommendations are to have the shared pool hit ratio above 98% and the data buffer hit ratio above 95%.

The most common problem that occurs when too much memory is allocated to the SGA is operating system memory paging and swapping. Swapping and paging occurs when application programs consume more memory than is currently available. The operating system starts to transfer blocks of memory to swap space on disk. If data in the swap space is needed, the operating system transfers data from memory to the swap space to make room and moves the needed data to memory (hence the term swap). All operating systems have commands to monitor paging and swapping operations.

There is another problem that can occur that is not related to paging and swapping. Over allocating memory to the shared pool may cause Oracle to spend too much CPU time controlling the large memory area. If you are experiencing poor performance problems, have high Oracle CPU utilization and a very large shared pool, you may want to decrease the shared pool size even if swapping and paging is not occurring.

Conclusion

Tuning Oracle can be a challenging task. Oracle provides the administrator with a host of tuning knobs that are used to tailor the Oracle database environment to meet an application's specific processing requirements. There is a bewildering array of tools and information that can be used to increase the performance of an Oracle database. A review of some of the more important points covered in this chapter should help:

- Once again, read the Oracle Tuning and Performance manuals.

- Learn how to use the toolset used for performance monitoring and performance problem identification. Learning how to read an explain plan and understanding the information contained in the v$ tables will give you a good start. Follow that with STATSPACK, Oracle Tuning Pack and the Oracle traces.

- Read Don Burleson's book on the STATSPACK utility. Read it, study it and you will become a STATSPACK expert.

- Identify the scope of the performance problem before you attempt to tune it.

- Keep an open mind. Do not let tunnel vision prevent you from evaluating all of the possible reasons for the poor performance.

- Start by monitoring the database at a high level and then continue to narrow the scope of your monitoring until you pinpoint the problem.

- Be careful with the analyze utility. Analyzing tables will most likely change query access paths.

- Don't use hints unless it is absolutely necessary. You are altering SQL to influence the optimizer. This may have a negative impact when the data, application or database release changes.

Now that we have covered the basics of backup and recovery and tuning and performance, let's move on to something new. Instead of focusing on a single topic, the next chapter contains information, hints, tips, tricks and techniques that are not related to any specific Oracle discipline.

Miscellaneous Oracle Information

CHAPTER 8

The following sections provide information on a wide range of topics. Information provided includes general hints and tips to simplify administrative tasks and information that, although important, didn't fit into any other section.

The Foot Rule of Thumb

The Foot Rule of Thumb is that there are no rules of thumb! Don't listen to industry pundits about their rules. Make your own rules. How do you do that? Test! Experiment! Learn! Afraid that performance will suffer if you place 6 columns in an index to obtain index-only access? Build the index, monitor on-line transaction performance and find out. The index 95/5 rule (don't build indexes on queries that retrieve more than 5% of the rows) is a high-level recommendation. It doesn't ring true in all cases. Every environment is different and there are no two workload mixes that are the same. I have seen queries return much higher percentages of rows through indexes and the queries performed flawlessly. Remember rules of thumb are just that, general recommendations.

Try different column combinations, multiple index usage, clustering changes, etc. When prototyping complex joins between several tables, build a set of indexes that favors one access path and test the queries in question. Drop the first set of indexes and create indexes that favor another access path (such as two different tables being joined first or a different join method being used) and test again. Build the different permutations of indexes that influence the optimizer to join a different set of tables first or allow different join types to be performed. Test each different access path and keep a performance history of each change that is made. The above hint may seem to be a time consuming process, but until you learn access paths this is the best approach to take. I have spent hundreds of hours working with access paths and if I could impart one sentence of wisdom, it would be the following one: What path works well in one situation may not be the best choice for another situation that almost exactly duplicates the first!

Create your own test instance and experiment. One of Oracle's great benefits is that it runs virtually anywhere. Create your own test environment. If you aren't sure how something works and the manuals aren't explicit enough, build a test case and execute it. I use my Oracle9i environment on a daily basis to teach others and continue my own database education.

Monitor By Day So You Don't Get Called at Night

Experienced database administrators are able to identify and prevent potential problems before they occur. Daily monitoring scripts that provide information on datafile freespace, extent growth, and disk space utilization help to reduce the number of night time calls.

Daily monitoring of performance statistics allows the DBA to tune proactively instead of reactively. Reviewing these reports daily will reduce the number of performance surprises that occur. The Internet is an endless source of tuning and monitoring scripts. Third-party books are also good sources. Find an author you like (my favorites are Burleson and anyone from TUSC) and implement the scripts they recommend. Tune and tweak them until the fit your own unique requirements. My own library is a hodge-podge of scripts from various authors.

Run the reports using SQL*Plus as the reporting tool. Don't underestimate the reporting capabilities that SQL*Plus provides. SQL*Plus reports can include report breaks, page breaks, sum commands, min commands, max commands, averages, total lines, subtotal lines, headers, footers, custom column headings and data manipulations. Do not underestimate the power that this tool provides. The SQL*Plus manual contain dozens of formatting and data manipulation commands to help you create custom reports.

The following information from the Oracle V$ performance tables and data dictionary tables provides a good foundation for daily proactive monitoring:

- Datafile freespace.
- Segments having extent sizes that are greater than 20.
- Segments that are 20 extents from reaching their *maxextent* size.
- Disk free space. A neat trick is to run SQL*Plus on the database server to create the reports and use the

HOST command to issue the operating system command that returns disk space information. This will include the disk space information in the SQL*Plus output.

- Views and stored procedures that have a status of 'INVALID' in *dba_objects*.
- Data buffer hit ratios.
- Shared pool reload statistics.
- Log buffer flushes.
- Datafile I/O.
- Sorts to memory vs. sorts to disk.
- Rollback/Undo performance indicators
- High resource consuming SQL statements.

Once you find the scripts that collect the aforementioned information, review them to see if they satisfy your needs, test and then implement them.

Use UNIX's CRON or the Windows platform AT scheduler to schedule the monitoring scripts to run during periods of low activity. Remember that data contained in the V$ tables is refreshed each time the database is started. As a result, performance statistics should be collected after the database has been active for a period of time (the longer the better). If performance information for a particular time period is required to solve a specific performance problem, administrators are able to use the BSTAT/ESTAT or STATSPACK utilities to collect the information.

Monitoring Space Utilization and Performance Statistics Historically

Monitoring space utilization and performance statistics historically provides the following benefits:

- Historical space tracking allows the DBA to determine table and index growth characteristics. The DBA is able to trend a particular data object's growth and size the data objects space utilization parameters accordingly.

- The DBA is able to trend space utilization in tablespaces. The DBA will be able to determine how quickly space is being consumed in the various tablespaces that make up the database. Tablespaces that are not growing quickly do not need as much free space allocated to them as their faster growing counterparts.

- Tracking tablespace growth allows the DBA to predict hardware upgrades months in advance.

- Tracking extent numbers historically allows the DBA to track fast growing objects.

- Tracking the various buffer hit ratios (data, shared pool, redo log), the number of active users and the number of reads and writes being performed in the system allows the DBA to trend database performance. The DBA will be able to track usage spikes. This will allow the DBA to forecast when performance will be good and provide a possible reason when performance degrades.

The following statements show you how to create a history table and then insert information into it. Run the insert script on a daily basis. It will give you and idea on how to create and load additional tables for performance stats (and whatever else you decide that is important to track historically). Hint: You may want to write PL/SQL to load some statistics into the performance tracker.

Creating the tracking tables:

```
create table system.extents_tracker (run_date date, tspace varchar2(30),
segtype varchar2(17), segowner varchar2(30),
segname varchar2(81), segext number, segbytes number,
seginit number, segnext number, segpctinc number)
tablespace tools storage (initial 50K next 50k pctincrease 0);
create table system.space_tracker (run_date date, tspace varchar2(30),
fileid number, maxspace number, minspace number, avgspace number, totspace number)
tablespace tools storage (initial 50k next 50k pctincrease 0);
```

Run these statements on a daily basis to update the tables:

```
insert into system.extents_tracker (run_date, tspace, segtype, segowner, segname, segext, segbytes, seginit, segnext, segpctinc) select sysdate, tablespace_name, segment_type, owner, segment_name, extents, bytes, initial_extent, next_extent, pct_increase from DBA_SEGMENTS where owner not in ('SYS', 'SYSTEM') and extents > 20;
insert into system.space_tracker (run_date, tspace, fileid, maxspace, minspace, avgspace, totspace)
select sysdate, tablespace_name, file_id ,
max (bytes) , min (bytes), avg (bytes), sum (bytes)
from sys.dba_free_space
where tablespace_name in (select tablespace_name from sys.dba_tablespaces)
group by sysdate, tablespace_name, file_id;
```

Run these statements to produce the historical tracking reports:

```
ttitle "Extents Tracker Reports"
set linesize 180
break on segtype skip 2
break on segname skip 2
column segname format a25
column tspace format a8
column segtype format a8
column segowner format a8
column segowner heading OWNER
column segext format 999
column segext heading EXT
column segbytes format 999,999,999
column seginit format 999,999,999
column segnext format 999,999,999
column segpctinc format 99
column segpctinc heading INC
select segname, run_date, segowner, segtype, tspace, segext,
segbytes, seginit, segnext, segpctinc
from extents_tracker
order by segname, segtype, run_date;
ttitle "Space Tracker Reports"
break on fileid on tspace skip 2
column tspace format a8
column fileid format 99
column maxspace format 9,999,999,999
column minspace format 9,999,999,999
column avgspace format 9,999,999,999
column totspace format 9,999,999,999
select tspace, fileid, run_date, maxspace, minspace, avgspace,
totspace from space_tracker
order by tspace, fileid, run_date;
```

Latches and Enqueues

What exactly is a latch? Oracle support describes latches as "low level serialization mechanisms used to protect shared data structures in the SGA. The implementation of latches is operating system dependent, particularly in regard to whether a process will wait for a latch and for how long." Its job is to prevent multiple processes from executing the same piece of code at the same time.

Enqueues, another locking mechanism employed by Oracle, allow several processes to share a single database resource. A process that wants to read a table issues a read table lock that allows other processes to access the table is a good example of an enqueue. An enqueue allows multiple processes to store the lock mode to provide varying degrees of sharing. Enqueues do not rely upon the database's internal locking mechanism to keep track of the locked resource, they instead use the operating system's locking mechanism to provide the sharing functionality. If a process has to wait because of an incompatible enqueue, the operating system will place the requesting process on a wait queue.

Deadlock Detection

Transaction deadlocks occur when two or more transactions are attempting to access an object with incompatible lock modes. The following script can be used to identify deadlocks in the database. The query depends upon objects that are created by the script $ORACLE_HOME/rdbms/admin/dbmslock.sql. Log on as SYS or with SYSDBA authority and run this script in all databases. You may have to run the deadlock monitoring script below numerous times before you identify the transaction that is causing the problem. A neat trick is to embed the script in a PL/SQL stored procedure that accepts command-line input parameters for the total number of runs and time intervals between runs. The output can be sent to a table or to an output datafile.

```
select dl.session_id, s.serial#, substr(dl.mode_held,1,4),
s.osuser,
o.owner,o.object_name, o.object_type, l.type from dba_objects o,
v$locked_object lo, v$lock l,dba_locks dl, v$session s
where lo.object_id=l.id1 and
lo.object_id=o.object_id
and dl.session_id = s.sid
and l.sid=s.sid
and blocking_others <> 'Not Blocking';
```

Unindexed Foreign Keys and Locking Problems

Prior to Oracle9i Release 2, unindexed foreign keys were a common cause of locking problems. To fully understand why this problem occurs, a brief introduction to referential integrity relationships is required.

A primary key constraint consists of one or more columns that uniquely identify a row in a table. A column that is a primary key cannot have duplicates or contain NULLs (lack of a value). A unique key constraint consists of one or more columns that enforce row uniqueness but the columns can contain NULLs. A table can only have one primary key or unique key defined.

The referential integrity relationship is established by creating a foreign key constraint on a table that points to or "references" the primary or unique key constraint in another table. The foreign key constraint declaration consists of: a constraint name (optional), the columns comprising the foreign key, a clause that references the table containing the primary or unique key constraint and a delete clause (discussed later).

The table being referenced by the foreign key is called the parent table while the table containing the foreign key is called the child or dependent table. The foreign key columns must match the primary key or unique key columns in number and should match the primary key or unique key column's datatypes and column lengths.

The following business rules are established when the foreign key is created:

- When inserting a row into the dependent table, Oracle identifies the contents of the foreign key columns and checks to see if a matching value exists in the parent table's primary key or unique key columns. If a matching value is not found in the parent table, the insert is rejected.

- When the columns comprising the foreign key are updated, Oracle performs the same check as when rows are being inserted.

- Deleting rows in the dependent table is permitted.

- When rows are deleted from the parent table, Oracle will search for foreign key values in the dependent table that match the deleted rows' primary key or unique key values. How Oracle handles parent table row deletes depends upon how the delete clause was specified during foreign key creation. Oracle will either set matching foreign key values in the dependent table to NULL, restrict deletion if rows having matching foreign key values are found or delete rows in the dependent table that have matching foreign key values.

- When the parent table's primary key or unique key is updated, Oracle will search the dependent table for foreign key values that match the value of the primary key or unique key being updated. If any matching values are found, Oracle will prevent the primary key or unique key from being updated.

The locking problem occurs when Oracle performs the foreign key search during parent table row deletions and primary key/unique key updates. If the foreign key is indexed, Oracle will use the index to perform the foreign key value search. The index columns must match the foreign key columns in order and in number (no additional columns can be contained in the index).

If no index is found, two events occur that are somewhat troublesome: Oracle will perform a table scan on the dependent table to identify matching foreign key values and in releases previous to Oracle9i Release 2, Oracle will issue a share lock on the entire dependent table while the foreign key search is being performed.

The table level share lock prevents transactions from completing DML operations on the child table until the foreign key search is complete. The table level share lock and the poor performance of the table scan combine to create an environment that is ideal for transaction deadlocks.

In Oracle9i Release 2, Oracle will issue and instantly release the table level share lock. This new locking strategy allows Oracle to identify any potential changes occurring on the child table, while the instant release means that DML can resume almost instantly once the parent table modification has started. If multiple rows are updated or deleted in the parent table, Oracle issues a share lock and release on the child table for each row being manipulated in the parent.

This new locking strategy does not completely solve the locking problem with unindexed foreign keys. It is highly recommended that indexes be created on all foreign keys that reference rows in parent tables that have the possibility of being accessed by update and delete statements.

Using PUPBLD

pupbld.sql can be used for more than stopping those irritating "PRODUCT PROFILE TABLE NOT LOADED" messages from occurring when you log on to SQL*PLUS. *pupbld.sql* creates a product profile table that is read by SQL*PLUS when users log on to the product.

Front-end applications can be designed to prevent users from updating data incorrectly. What happens if the user logs on to the database using their database account and password using SQL*PLUS? The application code is not available to prevent them from making incorrect or unwarranted changes to the database data. Administrators can prevent this from happening by inserting rows into the product profile table to disable a SQL*PLUS user's ability to execute:

- SQL*PLUS commands - COPY, EDIT, EXECUTE, EXIT, GET, HOST (or your operating system's alias for HOST, such as $on VMS, and ! on UNIX),QUIT, PASSWORD, RUN, SAVE, SET, SPOOL, START

- SQL statements ALTER, ANALYZE, AUDIT, CONNECT, CREATE, DELETE, DROP, GRANT, INSERT, LOCK, NOAUDIT, RENAME, REVOKE, SELECT, SET ROLE, SET TRANSACTION, TRUNCATE, UPDATE

- PL/SQL commands - BEGIN, DECLARE

- SQL*PLUS reads restrictions from *product_user_profile* when a user logs on using SQL*PLUS and maintains those restrictions for the duration of the session. To disable a SQL or SQL*PLUS command for a given user, insert a row containing the user's username in the USERID column, the command name in the ATTRIBUTE column, and DISABLED in the CHAR_VALUE column.

Copying databases between servers

Don't use the EXPORT/IMPORT utility to copy databases between servers running the same operating system. Execute the following steps to speed the transfer:

- Execute the ALTER DATABASE BACKUP CONTROLFILE TO TRACE statement on the source server.

- Bring the database down and copy the trace file, parameter file, all datafiles, control files and redo logs to the new server.

- Edit the trace file to change the database name if you need to (also change the REUSE keyword to SET), change NORESETLOGS to RESETLOGS, change directory names if they have changed, delete all comments and lines that have a # in front of them (they aren't comments in all tools).

- Connect internal and run the SQL statement contained in the trace file. It will start up the database in NOMOUNT stage and recreate the control files. The script will then MOUNT and OPEN the database.

Oracle9i - Resumable Space Allocation

Running update jobs that insert or update large amounts of data also cause their fair share of problems. Estimating the space required by large operations can be quite a formidable forecasting effort.

Do you add extra space to data and index tablespaces? Do you make the table and index INITIAL and NEXT extent sizes bigger? Do you increase the size of the rollback segments to handle the additional load? Should you increase the size of your TEMP tablespace and make your default INITIAL and NEXT extent sizes larger?

In previous releases, when an out of space condition occurred, the statement quit running and the database rolled back the unit of work. Rolling back can be a time-consuming (sometimes a VERY time-consuming) process. The DBA corrected the problem and the program was run again (hopefully successfully the second time). How many times have there been a third, fourth and fifth time?

Oracle 9i solves this problem with resumable statements. Oracle9i temporarily pauses SQL statements that suffer from out of space conditions (no freespace in tablespace, file unable to expand, maxextents or maximum quota reached). The DBA is able to easily identify the problem and correct the error. The statement will then resume execution until completion.

The ALTER SESSION ENABLE RESUMABLE statement is used to activate resumable space allocation for a given session. Developers are able to embed the

ALTER SESSION statement in programs to activate resumable space allocation. A new parameter, called RESUMABLE, is used to enable resumable space allocation for export, import and load utilities.

Statements do not suspend for an unlimited amount of time. A timed interval can be specified in the ALTER SESSION statement to designate the amount of time that passes before the statement wakes up and returns a hard return code to the user and rolls back the unit of work. If no time interval is specified, the default time interval of two hours is used.

When a resumable statement suspends because of an out of space condition, the following actions occur:

- A triggerable system event is initiated. Developers are able to code triggers that fire when a statement suspends.

- Entries are placed into system data dictionary tables. The data dictionary views *dba_resumable* and *user_resumable* can be accessed to retrieve the paused statement's identifier, text, status and error message.

- Messages are written to the alert log identifying the statement and the error that caused the statement to suspend.

The Oracle Database Fundamentals I (1Z0-031) certification test will have a few questions the new Resumable Space Allocation feature provided in Oracle9i. Test candidates should understand:

- Resumable Space Allocation basics and the benefits it provides

- What out of space conditions Resumable Space Allocation protects against
- The events that occur when a statement suspends
- The specifications used to configure Resumable Space Allocation

Oracle9i – Flashback Query

How many times have database recoveries been performed because of incorrect changes made to database data? Were your users ever unsure of the damage? There are times when a simple before change and after change comparison was all that was needed. If the damage was limited, a simple update may have been able to correct the problem. A process that is much less painless than a database restore.

Oracle9i's flashback query provides users with the capability of viewing data in the past. Oracle describes this new feature as "Oracle Invents the Time Machine" in many of its advertisements. It may not be a time machine, but it does allow data to be viewed in the past and it is easy to use. I must admit, I thought "It sounds too good. It has to be hard to use or not be reliable." I was wrong on both counts.

To take advantage of flashback queries, the database must use system managed undo segments. If flashback query is to be used, the administrator is tasked with determining how much of the old data should be kept available. The undo tablespace must be sized to hold the desired amount of undo data. Oracle documentation provides calculations that use update frequency and the amount of data being changed to estimate the required size of the undo tablespace.

The configuration parameter *undo_retention*, which specifies the amount of time that Oracle attempts to keep undo data available, plays an important role in flashback query. Although Oracle documentation recommends flashback query for applications that want to view data in the past, it is important to understand that the *undo_retention* parameter does not force Oracle to keep the old data in the undo tablespace. Depending on the available disk storage allocated to the undo tablespace, the database might not always be able to keep all of the requested undo data available. Providing active transactions with undo image space takes precedence over flashback query requirements. As a result, applications should not be designed to depend on the availability of historical data retrieved from undo segments.

The system supplied package *dbms_flashback* is used to provide flashback query capabilities. Standard date and time SQL functions can be used to determine the time in the past the data will be retrieved from. Here is an example that goes back five minutes:

```
EXECUTE DBMS_FLASHBACK.ENABLE_AT_TIME (SYSDATE - (5/(24*60)));
```

The above statement sends the session five minutes back in time for the duration of that session or until the EXECUTE *dbms_flashback.disable* is executed. Oracle recommends that the session not be ended without executing the *flashback.disable* procedure. I have seen a few sessions ended without executing *flashback.disable* without any detrimental affects. It is better to be safe than sorry, so the recommendation is to always execute *flashback.disable* before ending the session.

Currently, flashback query is able to provide 5 days (uptime not wall-clock) worth of data using the date and time parameter. To query data older than this, you must specify an SCN rather than a date and time. There are two important points to remember when using flashback query:

- The current data dictionary is used. If DDL changes have been made to the table between the time stated in the flashback query and the current point in time, an error will be returned.

- In Oracle9i Release 1, data cannot be updated during a flashback query enabled session. To save historical data, the old data can be placed into a cursor. The contents of the cursor can be dumped into a work table after the *flashback.disable* procedure is executed.

In Oracle9i Release 2, the AS OF *timestamp* clause has been added to the SELECT statement to enable flashback query on a specific table or set of tables. Developers are able to specify the AS OF clause for a single-table, multiple-tables (joins) as well as specify different times for different tables. The AS OF *timestamp* clause can also be used inside INSERT or CREATE TABLE AS SELECT statements.

Here is an example of a SELECT statement using the AS OF *timestamp* clause:

```
UPDATE emp.employee_payroll_table SET emp_salary =
       (SELECT emp_salary FROM emp.employee_payroll_table
```

```
                  AS OF TIMESTAMP (SYSTIMESTAMP - INTERVAL '1'
DAY)
                    WHERE emp_last_name = 'FOOT')
WHERE emp_last_name = 'FOOT';
```

The statement above uses the SYSTIMESTAMP value with an INTERVAL function to update the emp.employee_payroll_table with data that is 24 hours old.

The AS OF *timestamp* clause (and its *dbms_flashback.enable_at_time* counterpart) maps the timestamp value to a SCN value. Oracle records the SCN-TIMESTAMP mapping at 5-minute intervals. This means that the time you may actually retrieve the data from could be rounded down by up to 5 minutes. For example, you could access a table using a timestamp that is a few minutes after a table is created and receive an error because flashback query used a SCN value that is lower than the actual time when the table was created.

Remember, although flashback query is promising to be a beneficial feature in Oracle9i, it is not a panacea. Applications should not be designed to depend upon flashback query data. In addition, although it may prevent an occasional database recovery, it must be used cautiously. If data has been changed incorrectly, administrators must determine if other transactions have used that incorrect data as input. If the transactions using incorrect data as input have also made data changes, bad data is now being propagated throughout the database. It may be safer to perform a database recovery to a previous point in time.

Oracle9i – Flashback Query

The Oracle Database Fundamentals I (1Z0-031) certification test will have a few questions the new Flashback Query feature provided in Oracle9i. Test candidates should understand:

- The basics of the Flashback Query feature and the benefits it provides
- The feature's reliance upon automated undo management and the importance the *undo_retention* parameter has on Flashback Query
- How to use the DBMS_FLASHBACK package
- The impact DDL changes have on Flashback Query
- The use of the AS OF specification in SQL queries to activate the Flashback Query feature

Full Database Exports

When executing full database Exports, use CONSISTENT=Y to maintain a consistent view of the database. Oracle will ensure that all tables are consistent to the time the export utility started. Prevent "snapshot too old" messages by ensuring sufficient rollback/undo segments are available.

Large Table Imports

Use *commit*=Y on imports to reduce the chances of experiencing rollback/undo segment problems when importing large tables. The *commit*=Y parameter specifies whether Import should commit after each array insert. By default, Import commits only after loading each table. If an error occurs, Import will perform a rollback and continue with the next object. Specifying *commit*=Y prevents rollback segments from growing inordinately large and improves the performance of large imports.

Compressing Export Output Files in UNIX

If you are concerned about the size of your Export's dump file, you can use the following commands to create an Export dump file that is already compressed. Combining the Export and compress processes overcomes the requirement of creating the uncompressed dump file first and then compressing it later.

- Create the pipe - mknod expdat.dmp p
- Start the compress in background compress - < expdat.dmp > expdat.dmp.Z &
- Wait a second or two before kicking off the export - sleep 5
- Start the export - scott/tiger file=expdat.dmp

Terminating Oracle Processes (Threads) in Windows Systems

Oracle on NT provides the ORAKILL command to kill Oracle processes (called threads) in Windows systems. You need to specify the thread ID in Hex. Try orakill /? or orakill /h for more details.

Truncating vs Deleting

The Oracle load utility and SQL language have TRUNCATE commands that can be used to quickly remove data from Oracle tables. TRUNCATE

TABLE.......; is faster than the DELETE SQL statement and running a load with the TRUNCATE option specified is much faster than running the load utility with the REPLACE option. The TRUNCATE option is faster because it doesn't generate any undo information, does not fire DELETE triggers and does not record any information in the snapshot log. Since it does not generate undo, you cannot rollback the work to undo the removal of the data.

Copy Command in SQL*PLUS

Koch and Loney describe the COPY command as being "underutilized and unappreciated" in Oracle8I - The Complete Reference. The COPY command copies data from one table to another in the same or different databases. You are able to specify the columns to be copied, commit points (prevents those pesky rollback problems from occurring) and whether you want to append, create, insert or replace data in the target table. If you want to safely copy small to medium size tables between databases, try COPY.

Displaying Time in Milliseconds

You can use *dbms_utility.get_time* function to display the time in 100th of second

```
SELECT dbms_utility.get_time FROM dual;
```

!, $ and Host Command Differences

You can execute a "!" on UNIX and a "$" on MVS, VMS and Windows to execute operating system commands as child processes of SQL*PLUS. You can also execute the keyword "HOST" to do the same thing. What's the difference? "HOST" will perform variable substitution (& and && symbols), whereas "!" and "$" will not.

Learn Command Line BEFORE Using "Sissy GUI Tools" Like Oracle Enterprise Manager

Oracle Enterprise Manager may have a nice GUI interface, but it won't help you if you can't execute it. What happens when you get called at home or you don't have access to the GUI? Learn command line FIRST and then use OEM.

Don't Write Scripts

Don't write tuning, administration or monitoring scripts if you don't have to. The Internet has an abundance of web sites containing hundreds of scripts. Web sites to try first are www.orafans.com, www.tusc.com, or search the web using "oracle scripts" as the key word. Don't reinvent the wheel. Find a reputable site and save time.

Don't' Write Iterative SQL Statements – Generate SQL with SQL

If you need to perform the same alteration repeatedly, you may not need to code a specific statement to perform every change. You can use SQL to generate the statements for you. The statement below combines hard coded values with values returned from the database to generate an SQL statement that alters every user's default tablespace. The contents of that file can be used as input to SQL*PLUS.

```
spool 'c:\sql\output\alteruser.sql'
set verify off
set heading off
set echo off
set feedback off
set show off
set pagesize 0
set linesize 80
select 'alter user '||username||' default tablespace userwork;'
from dba_users;
spool off;
```

The statement above alters every user in the database to use the userwork tablespace as their default tablespace. The spool command writes the output to another file that will be used as input to SQL*PLUS to perform the alterations. The various set commands turns the display messages off so the output file can be executed in SQL*PLUS with little or no changes. The hard coded values 'alter user ' and 'default tablespace userwork;' will be included in every row of the result set. The pipe characters ("|"), tells SQL*PLUS to write the output values next to each other (a comma will cause SQL*PLUS to display 3 spaces).

Input Truncated to 9 Characters

Have you ever received that message in your SQL*PLUS output? Irritating, isn't it? Especially when you are using SQL to automatically generate other SQL. Place a carriage return after the last line of the statement or procedure. The message is gone!

Conclusion

The intent of this chapter was to provide readers with a general list of hints, tips and information on administering an Oracle database environment. A few of the topics covered bear repeating:

- Don't take rules of thumb as gospel. Databases are like fingerprints, they are all different and they will react differently to administrative changes. Make the desired change and test the results. Then develop your own rules of thumb.

- If you don't want to get called at night, you must monitor by day.

- Track free space and performance statistics daily to trend space utilization and database performance.

- Unless you have a lot of free time, don't code scripts. Scour the web and third-party books and modify them to fit your particular needs.

- Foreign keys that do not have indexes are common causes of Oracle performance and locking problems. It is highly recommended that indexes be created on all foreign keys that reference rows in parent tables that have the possibility of being accessed by update and delete statements.

- Oracle describes the new Oracle9i Flashback feature as the "Oracle Time Machine". It may not be a time machine, but it does allow data to be viewed in the past and it is easy to use.

- Use CONSISTENT=Y to maintain a consistent view of the database when executing full database Exports,

- Use COMMIT=Y on Imports to reduce the chances of experiencing rollback/undo segment problems when importing large tables.

The database administrator, because of his "general technical expert" title, is often asked to assist in the evaluation of third-party toolsets and applications. The next chapter discusses evaluating third party products.

Evaluating Third-Party Products

CHAPTER 9

As we learned previously, database administrators are much more than just "table jockeys." We often become involved in the evaluation of third-party business applications, application development tools and database administration and monitoring products. Over the years, I have developed a Product Evaluation Methodology that you may find helpful.

A methodology can be loosely defined as a body of practices, procedures and rules used to accomplish a given task. The task in this case is to evaluate and select information technology products. The success of any methodology depends on its continuous refinement. As a result, all methodology documents should be considered to be "work in progress." The steps contained in this section are not meant to be followed verbatim. They should be considered as a set of general recommendations to be used to increase the quality of the third-party application evaluation process.

Initial Analysis

Clarifying the business needs takes place during this phase. Individual, departmental and corporate requirements are evaluated. The focus of the analysis is on solving the business problem as opposed to buying a product. End users may have conflicting requirements. Needs clarification helps the users in synthesizing a common statement of the overall requirements. Analysis to determine if existing products can solve the problem is performed at this time. The make vs buy analysis is also completed during the initial analysis phase.

The following questions need to be addressed during the initial analysis:

- Can the solution be provided with existing product sets?
- Should the product be purchased or built in-house?
- Are other business or technology units able to utilize the product?
- Does the product provide any other additional benefits?
- What is the impact of not solving the business or technology problem?

Determine Impact to the Information Technology Support Infrastructure

The product's affect on the support infrastructure is determined during this phase. Although the major focus should be on solving the problem identified in the initial analysis, it is proper to allow external considerations to affect the final outcome. A product is useless if it cannot be successfully implemented and integrated into the existing information processing environment. The product's impact on individuals and groups as well as its impact on existing products and technologies is determined at this time.

Collect the following information during this phase of the analysis project:

- The use of new products often increases development time and training costs. Can the additional time and higher application development costs be justified by an increase in functionality or competitive advantage?

- If the product requires support from the development area, can the application personnel effectively administer the selected product?

- Risk vs Benefit. Is the additional functionality/competitive advantage worth any additional risk the product brings to the business or IT units? This is often described as the *comfort ratio*.

- Identify changes to the organizational infrastructure required to support the product (staff additions, training, etc.)

- Identify changes to other technologies and products.

- Identify additional products required to support the selected product.

- Identify changes to existing technologies and products the selected product will require.

- Identify changes to policies and procedures the selected product will require.

Analysis Evaluation

The analysis evaluation determines the resources required to evaluate, select, implement and support the selected product. Some problems may not be cost-effectively solved by existing technologies. Evaluation personnel must estimate the costs required to evaluate the competing products. In other words, don't spend $100,000 to evaluate a $1,000 product. As a rule of thumb, the evaluation, selection and procurement costs should range from three and ten percent of the project budget. The time required to perform the evaluation is also determined during this phase.

Perform the following activities during this phase:

- Determine and estimate the resources required to further evaluate the business needs.
- Determine and estimate the resources required to perform the product selection.
- Estimate general implementation and customization costs.
- Estimate on-going support costs, including staff requirements and training.
- Determine timelines and deliverables for the evaluation, selection and implementation processes.
- Determine date when the recommendation will no longer be valid (recommendation life-cycle).

Obtain Business Unit and IT Management Commitment

One of the major activities of any evaluation process is acquiring management commitment for the evaluation, selection and implementation stages. Representatives from user and technical management need to be a part of the evaluation process to ensure their continued support. Management always asks the same questions.

As a result, it is relatively easy to prepare for them. A satisfactory answer to "What business problem are you trying to solve?" is usually followed by "How much will it cost to purchase, implement and support?", and "What is the risk if we don't solve the problem?". Management wouldn't be doing their job if they didn't ask these questions. To be successful in this phase, you need to be prepared to answer them.

Obtain business unit and IT management commitment on the evaluation process, selection process and possible implementation by providing the following information:

- Reasons why you are performing the evaluation (What business problem are you trying to solve?)
- How the product solves the business problem.
- What you intend to test.
- Time and cost estimates for product selection, implementation and on-going support (Is the solution worth the cost?)

Create Evaluation Team

The evaluation team is created in this phase. For products that do not have a wide impact and are relatively inexpensive, the evaluation team will consist of a few select individuals. But for products that have a wide impact or are expensive, it is prudent to involve a larger group, some with a technical background, others with a user perspective. Wide representation and diverse viewpoints early in the decision process produce better decisions and fewer surprises later. It is imperative to include all those affected: IT personnel who will be supporting the product, IT groups affected by its usage and end-users. Team leaders are also identified during this phase.

The evaluation team consists of representatives from:

- Infrastructure support (personnel who are experienced in related technologies or who would be affected by the product implementation).
- Application developers who will be supporting the application.
- Business unit champions and end-users.

Locate Potential Vendors

Identifying the vendor offerings that will be evaluated takes place in this phase. The problem is usually too much information as opposed to too little. The best way to create a potential vendor list is to take a structured view of the marketplace and investigate all avenues to give your evaluation team the best possible chance of finding the alternatives.

A few sources of locating potential vendors follow:

- Internal personnel who are experienced in related technologies (evaluation team).
- Industry research groups- Gartner, GIGA, Burton, IDC.
- Internal research - trade journals and trade shows.
- Vendors that have existing relationships with your company (i.e. IBM, MSOFT, Oracle, etc.)
- Internet search engines.

Initial Elimination

This phase will eliminate products that should clearly not be considered as viable alternatives. The overall intent is to reduce the number of candidates being evaluated. With each additional candidate, the cost of the evaluation increases. The key to a successful elimination process is to create an in-depth set of evaluation criteria that will be used to evaluate the potential candidates. Using weighted measures helps to identify the measurement criteria that are most important to solving the business problem. If the product passes this phase, it is passed to the vendor evaluation phase for a more thorough examination.

Perform the following activities during this stage:

- Create the vendor selection process (methods used to perform the evaluation) and evaluation metrics (evaluation criteria used to compare the products). Document both the evaluation methods and metrics. The evaluation metrics will include:
    - Vendor Assessment (financial stability, size, alliances, etc.).
    - Functional requirements - evaluate product based on its ability to solve the business problem.
    - Technical requirements - evaluate product based on its technical capabilities.
- Create a general requirements document containing a compliance matrix that uses weighted measures to show how each vendor meets the requirements.

- Create and distribute a Request for Information (RFI) document using the evaluation metrics created above as the basis for the document.
- Evaluate the vendor responses to the Request for Information request.
- Reformulate the requirements based on vendor input.
- Create a vendor short list to keep evaluation costs to a minimum.

Vendor Evaluation

An in-depth evaluation of each of the remaining products takes place in this phase. The processes and methods created in this step are more detailed than those created in the initial elimination phase. Vendor responses to the Request for Information may also require alterations to both evaluation processes and evaluation metrics. Remember that any product is usually a compromise of function, speed and cost. You need to determine which factors are most important to you and weight them more heavily during your evaluation. A Request For Proposal (RFP) helps to formalize the evaluation process. The Request For Proposal details the scope of the sales process and defines the procedures and rules to be followed by the vendors. Vendors are more enthusiastic about committing resources to the sales process when it is clear to them how they are to respond and how their responses will be evaluated.

Perform the following steps in the Vendor Evaluation phase:

- Create a final vendor selection process (methods used to perform the evaluation) and weighted evaluation metrics (evaluation criteria used to compare the products).
    - The evaluation processes and metrics created in this phase are more in-depth than those created during the Initial Analysis phase.
    - Vendor responses to the Request for Information may require alterations to both evaluation processes and evaluation metrics.
    - Functional requirements – evaluate the product based on its ability to solve the business problem.
    - Technical requirements - evaluate the product based on its technical capabilities.
- Create Request for Proposal (RFP)
    - The Request for Proposal is more formal than the Request for Information.
    - The document details the scope of the sales process (meetings, presentations, product demos, trial periods, timelines and deliverables).
    - It also defines the procedures and rules to be followed by vendors during the evaluation process. Ground rules are written and shared with the qualified vendors.
    - Notify the vendors of how they will be evaluated (overview of compliance matrix).
- Vendor meetings and presentations are held during this phase.

- Create a questionnaire and contact the vendor supplied customer references.
- The evaluation matrix is used to measure product conformance to the business unit IT unit requirements.

Communicate Results

The results of the evaluation process are communicated during this phase. There are many communication avenues to choose from. A formal evaluation document is created and distributed. Presentations detailing the evaluation process are also given. Before you make your recommendation, be prepared to justify it. The major questions to ask yourself are "Did you choose the best product?", "Did you keep the level of risk at an acceptable level?" and "Did you achieve these objectives at a reasonable price?"

The documentation provided to business and IT management includes:

- An executive summary.
- A detailed description of the vendor chosen.
- A financial analysis of the chosen vendor
- The reasoning behind the vendor's selection.
- What other products were evaluated and the reasons why they weren't selected.
- An overview of the evaluation process.
- The metrics used as the basis for evaluation.

- An overview of the responses to the Request for Information and the Request for Proposal.
- The benchmark results of all competing products, if any.

Conclusion

This chapter provided an overview of the third-party product review process. Its intent was not to persuade readers into using the supplied review process verbatim. The information in this chapter rather should be used as the foundation for a strategy that is tailored to the individual needs of each shop's business and IT requirements. Some key points to remember from this chapter follow:

- Create an evaluation team that consists of all areas that will be using or supporting the product being evaluated.
- Determine the cost of the product and use it determine the cost of the evaluation project. Don't spend $100,000 dollars to evaluate a $5,000 product.
- The creation of a weighted vendor evaluation checklist is of utmost importance. It will help provide an un-biased, thorough evaluation of each vendor.
- Maintain good communications with the competing vendors. Treat them with respect and your company will deserve the good reputation it achieves.
- State the rules of the evaluation process (deadlines, number of copies of the RFP/RFI required, etc) clearly in all documentation. The vendors will usually give you everything you want, but you have to remember to ask!

- Find a champion in upper-management to help you achieve your desired goals.

- The more supporting documentation justifying the product you want and the vendor you have chosen, the easier it will be to obtain management concurrence.

- Be prepared from the beginning to tell management what problem it solves and how much it costs (they always seem to focus on those two issues first).

The next chapter could possibly be the most helpful one of all. It provides some general recommendations on optimizing Oracle administrative tasks.

Ease of Administration

CHAPTER 10

Successful database administration units understand that providing better support to their customers not only comes from advances in technology but also from innovations in human behavior. The selection of support-related technologies is important but it is the effective implementation and administration of those technologies that is critical to organizational success.

This section will provide some helpful information on improving the quality of database support activities. Because DBA responsibilities are dynamic and varied in nature, daily administrative tasks are sometimes given less priority than they deserve. Although some of the tips may seem obvious, the overall theme of this section is to reduce the time spent on daily administrative activities and increase the quality of day-to-day support.

Good Documentation is Essential

Documenting processes, procedures and best practices is a task that is often considered to be boring and mundane. Most DBAs would rather perform virtually any other activity than sit in front of a screen using a word processor. As a result, creating documentation is often postponed until the DBA has a little free time to kill. Today's database administration units are operating with smaller staffs, tighter budgets and ever-increasing workloads. The end result is that the documentation is either never created or created and not kept current.

But a robust detailed documentation library creates an environment that is less complex, less error-prone, reduces the amount of time DBAs spend learning new database environments and reduces the overall time spent on day-to-day support activities. DBAs are able to spend more time administering the environment than finding the objects they are trying to support.

The following list of suggestions will provide a good foundation for any database administration library:

- Naming conventions
- Servers
- Databases
- Tablespaces
- Datafiles – naming conventions should allow the relationship between tablespaces and tablespace datafiles to be easily recognized (i.e. the first datafile for tablespace empindex would be empindex_01.dbf).
- Rollback segments (if undo segments aren't used)
- Online redo logs
- Tables
- Indexes
- Users
- Views
- Clusters

- Constraints
- Roles
- Profiles
- Outlines
- Materialized views
- Directories containing application program code
- Stored PL/SQL programs
- Sequences
- Database links
- Tnsnames alias entries
- Administrative support script directories divided into the following sub-directories
    - Day-to-day support scripts
    - Monitoring scripts
    - Backup scripts
    - Scripts used to perform database changes
- Administrative support scripts
- Administrative support script output directories.
- Administrative script output and report files. Each output file and report name should include the execution date.
- Archive logs and archive log destination directories
- Backup directories for hot and cold backups
- Backup program output
- Export output directories

Good Documentation is Essential

- Export control cards
- SQL*Loader control cards
- SQL*Loader output files
- Export output files
- Anything else that is created on a regular basis
- Database environmental information
- Operating system type and release
- Database release
- Application type (i.e. data warehouse, online transaction processing, decision support, third-party application name and functionality it provides).
- Number of users
- General estimation of disk space consumed
- A daily monitoring activity checklist to ensure that no activity is missed
- Review space reports (i.e. freespace, extents, mountpoints, directories)
- Review performance reports
- Review output from backup process execution
- Review output from data loads (SQL*Loader, custom programs)
- Review alert log and trace files for errors
- Review output from auditing
- Complex administrative activities performed regularly
- Test and reporting database refreshes
- Data reorganizations

- Database test recovery procedures
- Disaster recovery test procedures
- Business unit requirements and related information for supported databases
- Uptime requirements (i.e. 24 X 7, 8 X 5)
- Database downtime windows
- Critical job processes
- Business unit and application developer contact lists
- Turnover windows for database changes
- Problem notification and escalation procedures
- Database administration unit contact information and support escalation procedures It is a good practice to distribute this information to all business units supported by the database administration unit.

Follow OFA Naming Conventions

OFA stands for Optimal Flexible Architecture. The OFA standard is a set of naming conventions and configuration guidelines that:

- Distributes I/O among different disk drives.
- Facilitates ease of administration by creating naming conventions for mountpoints, directories, file suffixes, database binary directories and database output (i.e, background dump, cored dump).

These standard naming conventions and placement guidelines are intended to improve database performance by spreading I/O, protect against drive failures and also allow administrators to more easily

Follow OFA Naming Conventions **261**

assume the responsibility of supporting new database environments. In addition, because OFA standards are well documented by the Oracle Corporation, newly hired DBA and consultants are able to more quickly assume administration responsibilities.

Proceduralize Administrative Support for the Application Development Process

One of the first sections of this booklet provides information on database design reviews. Database design review meetings foster effective communications between the DBA unit, system support personnel and application developers throughout the entire application design and implementation process. When Oracle design issues are addressed early in the development lifecycle, problems are minimized and the migration from test to production is more easily accomplished.

Proceduralize the Change Request Process

Database administrators usually support different business units with each unit having their own set of procedural requirements. Formalizing and documenting the change request process minimizes the potential for miscommunication between the business units, application development areas and the database administration unit.

The notification lead-time required for the database administration team to perform a requested change should be documented and distributed to business and application development units. This will prevent your team for getting a request to migrate a database from test to production in the morning with a required date for that afternoon. Of course we all know that never happens.

Standardized request documents also help to increase the quality of the change request process. The forms are sent to the database administration unit by the business unit owner of the data to be processed. Any requests not sent or signed off by the data owner should be rejected. Keep copies of all completed work requests for auditing purposes.

Each request form contains the following common information:

- Application name
- Database name
- Name and contact information of the person requesting the change
- Request date
- Required date
- Data owner signoff signature
- Data security signoff signature
- A free form request area for non-standard requests
- An area that the DBA will fill out when executing the change that contains the following information:
- DBA executing change.
- DBA contact information.
- Date and time change was processed.
- Verification procedures followed.

Here are a few examples of specific forms that will help formalize the change request process:

- **Oracle Authorization Request Form** – used for requesting authorization changes to the Oracle database environment.

  The Oracle Authorization Request Form contains the following information pertinent to Oracle authorization requests:

  - Grantee listing for security grant or revoke.
  - Type of security granted or revoked.

- **Oracle Database Change Request Form** – used for requesting physical changes to the Oracle database environment. The form will be used for requesting both system changes (i.e. modifying rollback segments, temporary tablespaces, default tablespaces) and object changes (adding new columns, creating new indexes, etc.).

  The Oracle Database Change Request Form contains the following information pertinent to Oracle change requests:

  - Schema owner of object to be changed.
  - Object name to be changed.
  - Object type (i.e. table, index, view) of the object to be changed.
  - Detailed description of change requested.

- **Oracle Migration to Production Request Form** - used for requesting the migration of Oracle objects (databases, tablespaces, tables, indexes, etc.) from test to production.

The Oracle Migration to Production Form contains the following information pertinent to the object migration process:

- o Object name of the object to be migrated.
- o Object type for the object to be migrated.
- o The name of the database the object will be migrated from (source database).
- o The name of the database the object will be migrated to (target database).
- o A freeform area for special processing required during the migration process.

Create and Standardize Monitoring and Administration Scripts

All DBAs have their own set of favorite Oracle administration and monitoring scripts. They find them on the web, get them from third-party books and trade them like bubble-gum cards. They then tune, tweak and tailor them until they fit their own unique style of administration.

It is highly recommended that database administration units create a set of scripts for daily monitoring, hot and cold backups, exports and common administrative activities. This library of scripts can then be installed on each server administered by the team. Personalizing the scripts should be highly discouraged. Any modifications to the library can be reviewed during team meetings. Assign a team member the responsibility of being the script library owner. The script library owner will be responsible for making all script modifications and installing the new scripts on the supported servers.

Repeatable Processes

Repetition, even though it can be boring, is the foundation for a high quality support environment. If the scripts and administrative process worked correctly the first time, chances are they will continue to work correctly in the future.

Documenting complex administrative processes such as production to decision support database refreshes and application upgrade activities will allow future iterations of these activities to be executed more quickly and with less errors.

Create Service Level Agreements

Identifying support needs and expectations is required to provide high quality support. You probably won't be meeting all of your customer's expectations if you don't know what any of them are. As stated previously, each application has it own unique set of support requirements and expectations. Service Level Agreements (SLA) help to solidify support requirements and dispel any inflated expectations a business or application development unit may have. They probably won't be aware of your current workload and resulting work request lead times until you tell them. The DBA team lead should meet with each unit supported to establish a set of measurable Service Level Agreements that include work request lead times, support activities required and application performance and availability objectives.

DBA Report Cards and the 360-Degree Review Process

Effective measurements are required to judge the success of any activity. The quality of support the DBA team provides needs to be reviewed on a regular basis. A DBA report card allows business and application development units to provide feedback on DBA support activities. The report card will allow them to measure how well they feel you are meeting your Service Level Agreement objectives.

Meetings can be held with the respondents to discuss their reviews. DBA team members participating in the reviews must be prepared to respond to criticism in a professional manner. But just as its title describes, the 360-degree review process also allows support units to provide feedback on their customer support requests and work activities. The 360-degree review process provides important feedback to both support units and their customers. Once again, your customers may not know that some of their expectations are unachievable until you tell them the reasons why.

Corrective Action Reports

Oracle is a challenging database to administer. As much as we would like to prevent all of our mistakes, we do make them. A corrective action document provides your customers with the information they need to understand what happened and how you will prevent if from occurring again. The document will help you to not make the same mistake twice and also help to restore your customer's confidence.

The corrective action report should contain:

- A detailed description of the error that caused the problem.
- A timeline of the activities that were executed.
- The steps that were take to correct the problem.
- The steps that will be taken to prevent the problem from occurring again.

Conclusion

Administering an Oracle database environment requires dozens of different support activities to be performed on a daily basis. The more structured and formalized the support activities are, the fewer problems they cause. A review of some of the important points covered in this chapter follows:

- Don't skimp on documentation. It may be boring, but it is important. A robust, detailed documentation library creates an environment that is less complex, less error-prone, reduces the amount of time DBAs spend learning new database environments and reduces the overall time spent on day-to-day support activities.
- Design and implement standardized work request documents to increase the quality of the change request process.

- Repeatable processes reduce the level of administrative errors. If a set of steps works right one time, there is a good chance that it will work correctly the next.
- The more complex a particular task is the greater the need for thorough documentation.
- Internal service level agreements help database administration teams understand what their customers expect from them.

In our last chapter, we discuss Oracle security.

Oracle Database Security

CHAPTER 11

Securing an Oracle database environment requires more than just issuing SQL grant and revoke statements. The information in this section is by no means intended to be a thorough discussion of securing an Oracle database installation. Rather, it is intended to provide readers with a few helpful hints and tips that may protect your environment from unwanted access.

If you need to tightly secure a particular database environment, search the Internet for information using the keywords "Oracle Security." You will find dozens of websites that contain information on hacking and securing Oracle databases. Good sources of information are data security consultancy websites. These websites contain numerous presentations and documents on Oracle security issues.

Protecting Data Requires More than just Protecting the Production Database

If you remember anything from this discussion on Oracle security, make it the next sentence. Experienced hackers understand that they don't have to hack into your production database to access your production data.

Hackers often look for data in places that are left unsecured. The listing below provides a few examples of the data stores that hackers may access to steal your production data:

- Oracle Export utility output files. Oracle Export files can be easily transferred to a remote location and quickly loaded into any Oracle database to recreate your production database environment. The hacker then has unlimited access to all of your trade secrets in complete anonymity and without maintaining a connection to your production database.

- The file copies from hot and cold database backups. We (and the hackers) know that database backups are duplicates of your production database. It is a often a simple process for hackers to find the output files or find the scripts that create the backups for your production database environment.

- QA, test, development, reporting and disaster recovery databases. How many times have you been asked to refresh these non-production databases with production data? Once the data is refreshed, these non-production databases must be treated as production data stores and secured accordingly.

- Using LOGMINER to scan Oracle online and archived redo logs. Now that Oracle has provided us with a quick and easy way to access data changes stored in the redo logs, these files, and the LOGMINER utility, also needs to be secured.

- The UTL_FILE_DIR directories. UTL_FILE_DIR is used as the target directory for flat file output created from PL/SQL stored programs. Hackers can gain access to the parameter file that defines the output directory and gain access to the PL/SQL output.

Protecting Data Requires More than just Protecting

Identifying Granted Privileges

The Oracle database provides numerous ways of granting privileges to a user. A user can be granted those privileges specifically, or they can be granted a group of privileges contained in a database role. Roles can also be granted groups of privileges from other roles. In addition, Oracle users can also be granted default database privileges when they log on to the operating system containing the Oracle database. It is critical to investigate all of the potential ways a user can be granted security when attempting to protect an Oracle database environment.

The list below will help you in identifying what privileges users have in your database:

- *dba_users* – dictionary table listing all of the users created in the database.
- *dba_col_privs* – dictionary table listing all column-level grants in the database.
- *dba_tab_privs* – dictionary table listing all object grants in the database.
- *dba_sys_privs* – dictionary table listing all system grants in the database.
- *dba_roles* - dictionary table listing all ROLEs created in the database.
- *dba_role_privs* - dictionary table listing all ROLEs granted to users and other roles.
- *role_tab_privs* - dictionary table listing all object grants granted to ROLEs.

- *role_sys_privs* - dictionary table listing all system grants granted to ROLEs.
- *role_role_privs* – dictionary table listing all ROLEs granted to other ROLEs.
- *queue_privs* – dictionary table listing all privileges granted on queues for Oracle's advanced queuing option.
- *session_privs* – dictionary table listing all privileges currently active for a particular session.
- *session_roles* - dictionary table listing all ROLEs currently active for a particular session.
- *proxy_users* – dictionary table listing all users who have the capability of assuming the identity of other users.
- /etc/passwd – UNIX/LINUX system file that lists usernames, passwords and groups. In releases previous to Oracle9i, users that are members of the Oracle group have unlimited access to all databases on the server.
- /etc/group – UNIX/LINUX system file that lists all groups created in the operating system.
- Windows systems provide a user admin panel that lists the users and groups created in the operating system. As with its UNIX/LINUX counterparts, users that are members of the Oracle group have access to all databases on the server.

The Oracle Database Fundamentals I (1Z0-031) certification test will have a few questions on the tables used to identify what security is granted in an Oracle database. Test candidates should have a general understanding of the tables listed above.

Identifying Granted Privileges

Accounts Created During Database Creation

Depending on the options installed in the database, Oracle can contain up to 5-dozen additional accounts in the database. Oracle9i locks many of these accounts when they are created, requiring the administrator to unlock them before they can be used. In previous releases, these accounts are active when they are created. Some of these accounts may have high levels of privileges granted to them (including DBA). In addition, these accounts are often created with accountname=password name for ease of use.

Part of my responsibilities at Contemporary Technologies is to perform database audits for companies who want to increase the quality of their database environments. A series of scripts are executed in the database to gather information on key database statistics and structural information. Support personnel interviews are conducted to review administrative practices and procedures. The 200-point database assessment focuses on the database disciplines of data security, performance, reliability/availability, backup/recovery and data integrity. The current track record for passing the security section of the audit is pretty dismal. 80% of the databases reviewed fail the security audit because Oracle's default accounts are left unprotected.

The list below provides some of the more common accounts that could exist in the Oracle database (it's a good idea to review all of their authorities):

- system/manager – administrative account with DBA privileges. The Oracle9i Release 2 installer forces this account's password to be changed.
- sys/change_on_install – administrative account with DBA privileges. SYS also owns the data dictionary tables. The password provides a hint on what to do after the database is installed.
- scott/tiger, HR/HR, OE/OE, SH/SH – accounts that own test/demonstration tables in the Oracle database.
- ctx/ctx – ConText cartridge administrative account. Granted DBA privileges.
- mdsys/mdsys – spatial option administrator. Granted all privileges.
- outln/outlln – stored outlines for optimizer plan stability.
- dsnmp/dbsnmp – Oracle intelligent agent.
- aquser/aquser and aqdemo/aqdemo – accounts that are used for the advanced queueing option.
- ordplugins/ordplugins – object relational data used by spatial, time series, etc.
- auroraorbunauthenticated/invalid- users who do not authenticate using in Aurora/ORB.
- fnd/fnd, gl/gl, ar/ar, ap/ap, etc. – Oracle E-Business Suite applications create another entire list of accounts that own the data structures. The applications provide a security panel that allows administrators to change these passwords. A hacker's dream unless you secure all of them.

Accounts Created During Database Creation

Wrapping PL/SQL Programs

Oracle provides a stand-alone utility that encrypts PL/SQL programs stored in the Oracle database. Once the PL/SQL is encrypted, it cannot be read ensuring that competitive business logic is secure. The PL/SQL is encrypted before it is stored in the Oracle database. Companies that create third-party applications can use the wrap utility to deliver business logic to customers without exposing the source code.

Oracle wraps all of their supplied packages. If you want to see an example of wrapped PL/SQL source code, select the text from DBA_SOURCE for any of the Oracle supplied packages such as DBMS_OUTPUT.

The following command is used to wrap PL/SQL source code

```
wrap iname=script.sql
```

Where *script.sql* is the PL/SQL source code. Oracle will create an output file called *script.plb*. The output file is then executed to store the encrypted code in the Oracle database.

Using OPS$ Accounts

Administrators often use the OPS$ account to simplify Oracle security. The OPS$ account is created in the database and is used in conjunction with the *init.ora* parameter *remote_os_authent* to provide operating system authorization.

If *remote_os_authent* is set to TRUE, OPS$ accounts are authenticated by the operating system. Once the OPS$ user successfully logs into the operating system by supplying a valid account/password combination, they are able to connect to the database by using a "/" instead of a password.

A problem can occur in windows environments. Users that know an account that has OPS$ capabilities could change the name of their PCs to that account name and access the database remotely in SQL*Plus without supplying a password.

The Oracle Database Fundamentals I (1Z0-031) certification test may have a question on the OPS$ account feature. Test candidates should know the following information:

- The basics of OS authentication and the benefits it provides

- The different specifications for the *os_authent_prefix* initialization parameter and the effect they have on user logon

Using Security Profiles

Administrators are able to set account level security policies through the use of database profiles. Once the security profile is created with the CREATE PROFILE command, the administrator is able to use the CREATE USER or ALTER USER command to assign the security profile to the user.

Oracle profiles were initially used to set performance thresholds for Oracle users in the database.

Performance settings (CPU utilization, disk reads, idle time) were used to ensure that no single user dominated finite system resources. Oracle enhanced the profile to include security policies. All profile parameters that are not explicitly set in a user's customized profile (profiles aren't required to create a user) will default to the settings contained in the default profile (which are all set to unlimited). Each user is able to have only one profile assigned to them.

The following parameters help to establish a security policy for a given user:

- *failed_login_attempts* – the number of failed login attempts before the account is locked.

- *password_life_time* –the number of days before a password expires.

- *password_reuse_time* – the number of days before a password can be reused.

- *password_reuse_max* – the number of password changes required before a password can be reused.

- *password_lock_time* – the number of days an account will be locked after exceeding the number specified by *failed_login_attempts*.

- *password_grace_time* – the number of days after the grace period begins during which warnings are issued notifying the user that the password must be changed. The account will be locked after exceeding the number of days specified by this parameter.

- *password_verify_function* - the password complexity verification script.

Administrators using profiles to establish security policies must provide a mechanism for the user to change their passwords. If the user does not have access to SQL*Plus or a custom form in their application that allows them to change their passwords, they will be unable to change them.

The Oracle Database Fundamentals I (1Z0-031) certification test will have a few questions on the Oracle security profiles. Test candidates should know the following information:

- The basics of user security profiles and the benefits it provides
- How to create and alter security profiles
- How to assign security profiles to Oracle accounts
- How the default profile is used when an Oracle account does not have a value set in their assigned profile

SYS and SYSTEM Passwords

In Oracle9i Release 2, SYS and SYSTEM account default passwords can now be set at database creation time. Two new clauses have been added to the CREATE DATABASE statement to allow administrators to set SYS and SYSTEM passwords. The example shows the two new clauses in use:

```
CREATE DATABASE orcl
USER sys IDENTIFIED BY oracle
USER system IDENTIFIED BY rules;
```

The clauses are not mandatory in Oracle9i Release2 but you can't specify just one of them. You must specify the syntax for both clauses to successfully execute the CREATE DATABASE statement.

The Database Configuration Assistant (DBCA) is enhanced in Oracle9i Release 2 to persuade (read that force) administrators to change SYS and SYSTEM passwords during database creation. A security panel appears during DBCA execution that asks the user to set the SYS and SYSTEM password to non-default values. An error message will be returned if you use select MANAGER for SYSTEM or CHANGE_ON_INSTALL for SYS.

GRANT ANY OBJECT Privilege

In all releases prior to Oracle 9i Release 2, administrators wanting to grant object privileges on an object owned by another user were required to either:

- Log on as the object owner and grant the privilege to the grantee.

- Log on as the object owner, grant the desired privilege to their own account using the WITH GRANT OPTION clause. This would allow the administrator to then grant that privilege to others.

In Oracle9i Release 2, the GRANT ANY OBJECT privilege allows users to grant privileges on objects owned by another user. This privilege is granted to the user SYS and the DBA role by default. Saying that this feature has been a long-time coming is like saying the Titanic sprung a small leak.

Administrative User Auditing

When connecting to a database using the AS SYSDBA or AS SYSOPER attributes, the administrator is actually connected as SYS behind the scenes. To test this feature, perform the following exercise:

- Log on to the database as SYS/password as SYSDBA.
  ```
  SQLPLUS /NOLOG
  CONNECT sys/change_on_install AS SYSDBA;
  ```

- Create an account and grant that account the SYSDBA privilege.
  ```
  CREATE USER test IDENTIFIED BY test;
  GRANT sysdba TO test;
  ```

- Login using the new account and activate the SYSDBA privilege as you do so.
  ```
  CONNECT test/test AS SYSDBA;
  ```

- Execute the following statement to find out what account you are logged in as.
  ```
  SQL> SELECT USER FROM DUAL;
  USER
  ------------------------------
  SYS
  ```

Logging in as SYS or activating SYSDBA and SYSOPER during login enables the user to perform virtually any administrative function in Oracle. Oracle9i Release 2 enables the auditing of the activities performed when a user logs in as SYS or activates the SYSDBA or SYSOPER privilege during login.

Administrators activate administrative user logging by setting the new static initialization parameter *audit_sys_operations* to TRUE. This begins logging all SYS user operations to the operating system file that contains the audit trail. These actions cannot be logged to the SYS.AUD$ auditing table.

Administrators set the static initialization parameter *audit_file_dest* to specify which directory will store the auditing files. Administrators working in Microsoft Windows environments should note that *audit_file_dest* cannot be set on those platforms. By default, all audit files on Windows platforms will be sent to the APPLICATION log.

The *audit_trail* static initialization parameter will continue to be used to send other audited activities to the operating system (*audit_trail*=OS) or to the *sys.aud$* auditing table (*audit_trail*=DB).

Moving the AUD$ Table

Besides being known as a high resource consumer, auditing can also consume large amounts of disk space to hold the output it generates. If *audit_file_dest*=DB is specified in the Oracle *init.ora* parameter file, audit records will be sent to the *sys.aud$* auditing table. The *sys.aud$* is stored in the system tablespace by default.

The *sys.aud$* audit trail table will continue to grow unchecked unless it is deleted or truncated. Because *sys.aud$* grows and shrinks, it may cause fragmentation in the system tablespace. In addition, audit trail information being written to the system tablespace may drive the system tablespace's I/O to unacceptable levels.

Although not officially supported by Oracle, administrators are able to move *sys.aud$* to another tablespace. The administrator can create a tablespace to hold *sys.aud$* and use the ALTER TABLE MOVE command to move the table from the system tablespace to the new audit trail tablespace. The script that creates the *sys.aud$* table can also be modified to create *sys.aud$* in another tablespace during database creation.

The Oracle Database Fundamentals I (1Z0-031) certification test will have a few questions on auditing. Test candidates should have a strong understanding of:

- Auditing basics
- Auditing levels
    - Statement level auditing
    - User level auditing
    - Privilege level auditing
- How to send audit output to the operating system and Oracle tables
- The tables used to hold audit trail information

Conclusion

Database administrators, by the very essence of their job descriptions, are the protectors of their organization's core data assets (much to the chagrin of most corporate data security units). The Oracle Corporation provides a wealth of information on security on its Metalink (http://metalink.oracle.com) and Technet (http://technet.oracle.com) websites. In this last chapter, we covered the following topics:

- Hackers don't need to access your production database to steal your production information. Protect test databases refreshed from production, database backups and export output files. These data stores contain production data and must be secured accordingly.

- Oracle8i (and earlier releases) contain accounts that have high-level privileges granted to them and are activated during database creation. Many of these accounts are created with accountname=passwordname for ease of use. Change these passwords immediately after creating the database.

Certification Test Preparation

CHAPTER 12

Introduction

Getting certified is essential to career success for all Oracle database administrators. Certifications are especially important to those seeking employment in a field that often has many candidates competing for a single DBA position. An Oracle certification shows the potential employer that the candidate has made the commitment to "learn their trade" and has the background and education to quickly become a productive member of the DBA unit.

The Oracle Certification also gives a distinct advantage to DBAs looking to advance in their careers. Being an Oracle Certified Professional raises their visibility in the organization, which is a requirement for career advancement in most organizations. Employers want employees to distinguish themselves

The remainder of this chapter will provide information that OCA and OCP candidates need to know to successfully pass the certification tests. The intent of this chapter is to provide a general description of the topics that should be studied for each test. It is not intended to provide all of the necessary details to understand that particular item. The Oracle reference manuals, third-party books and Oracle classroom workbooks can be used to learn the information required to successfully understand each of the topics provided below. Use this chapter as a general guide to ensure that no areas are missed during test preparation.

Oracle Certified Associate Tests

Exam 1Z0-007 – Introduction to Oracle9i SQL

The first certification test covers the Oracle architecture and the SQL programming language. Students are taught how to create basic Oracle data objects and store and manipulate data using the SQL language.

The certification test covers the following topics:

1. Basic SQL statements
   a. INSERT
   b. UPDATE
   c. DELETE
2. Limiting data output using the WHERE CLAUSE
3. Sorting data output using the ORDER BY CLAUSE
   4. Table joins
      a. Inner join
      b. Outer join
      c. Full table join
   5. Single column functions.
      a. Character functions
      b. Number functions
      c. Date functions

d. Oracle9i date/time functions

6. Grouping data using the GROUP BY and HAVING clause

7. Subqueries

    a. Single-row subqueries

    b. Multiple-row subqueries

    c. Understand how to use EXISTS and NOT EXISTS

8. Using ISQL*PLUS to format report output

    a. ISQL*PLUS basics

    b. Customizing the ISQL*PLUS environment

    c. Creating and building ISQL*PLUS script files

9. Oracle Tables

    a. Creating tables

    b. Describing tables

    c. Altering tables

    d. Understanding Oracle table datatypes

10. Oracle Indexes

    a. Creating indexes

    b. Single and multiple column indexes

    c. Reverse indexes

    d. B-Tree indexes

    e. Bitmap indexes

11. Basic Oracle schema security

    a. GRANT

b. REVOKE

   c. Understand how ROLEs are used to simplify database security

12. Have a basic understanding of how Oracle database constraints are used to enforce business rules

13. Have a basic understanding of Oracle external tables

14. There always seems to be a few questions on hierarchical queries

Exam 1Z0-031 – Oracle Database Fundamentals I

Oracle Database Fundamentals I teaches students the fundamentals of basic database administration. Students learn the basic Oracle database architectural components including memory structures, background processes, database datafiles, control files and redo logs. Parameter file and password file management is also taught. The student also learns how to create Oracle database objects including databases, tablespaces, tables, views and indexes. Database constraints, security, auditing and NLS support is also covered. The certification test covers the following topics:

1. Oracle SGA components

   a. Shared pool

      i. Data dictionary cache

      ii. Library cache

   b. Data buffer cache

   c. Redo log buffer

d. Large pool

   e. Java pool

2. Server processes.

   a. PGA components

3. Background processes. Make sure you understand what each background process does and how they interrelate. You also need to understand what triggers DBWR, ARCH and CHKPT.

   a. SMON

   b. PMON

   c. DBWR

   d. LGWR

   e. ARCH

   f. CHKPT

   g. RECO

4. Database Files

   a. Tablespace data files

   b. Online redo logs

      i. Multiplexing

      ii. Sizing

      iii. Administering redo log groups

         (1) Adding redo log groups

         (2) Adding members to existing groups

         (3) Dropping redo log groups

         (4) Dropping members from existing groups

  iv. Log Switches. Understand what happens when a log switch occurs.

 c. Control files

  i. Multiplexing

  ii. Contents

  iii. Know how to retrieve information from the control files

5. Database SQL statement processing. Make sure you have a firm understanding of the sequence of events that occurs when a SQL statement is executed. Understand the processing that occurs when a transaction issues a COMMIT and a ROLLBACK.

6. Oracle Universal Installer

7. General Oracle Enterprise Manager Architecture

8. Database Startup. Know what happens during each stage of the startup process.

 a. NOMOUNT

 b. MOUNT

 c. OPEN

9. Database Shutdown Options. Know what happens to in-flight (active transactions when a particular shutdown option is used.

 a. SHUTDOWN NORMAL

 b. SHUTDOWN IMMEDIATE

 c. SHUTDOWN TRANSACTIONAL

 d. SHUTDOWN ABORT

10. Know the general concepts of OFA.
11. Data dictionary and dynamic performance tables. Know at which stage of startup the dictionary tables and dynamic views can be accessed.
12. Tablespaces and datafiles
    a. Types of tablespaces
        i. Rollback/undo
        ii. Temp - Know what a default temporary tablespace is used for and how it impacts temporary tablespace administration.
        iii. System
        iv. Data
    b. Understand the differences between locally managed and dictionary managed tablespaces.
    c. Know the steps to migrate a system tablespace from dictionary to locally managed.
    d. There will be a lot of questions on read only tablespaces
    e. Enabling automatic extension of datafiles
    f. Adding datafiles to an existing tablespace
    g. Know how to move online and offline datafiles
    h. Dictionary tables used to find tablespace information
13. Segment and extent administration
    a. Types of segments
        i. Rollback/Undo
        ii. Temporary

  iii. Data

 b. Know the storage clause precedence (object, tablespace, database)

 c. Extent allocation and deallocation

 d. The highwater mark

 e. Understand the contents of an Oracle block

 f. Standard and non-standard blocksizes

 g. Block freespace management

  i. Manual space management

   (1) PCTFREE/PCTUSED

   (2) Freelists

   (3) Freelist groups

  ii. Automatic segment management

 h. Dictionary tables used to find information on segments and extents

14. Managing Rollback/Undo data

 a. Understand the three uses of rollback segments

  i. Transaction rollback

  ii. Transaction recovery

  iii. Read consistency

 b. Know the concepts of automated undo management (Oracle9i)

 c. Know how to use the v$ tables to size the undo tablespace

15. Managing Oracle data objects

 a. Tables

      i. Datatypes

      ii. ROWID formats

      iii. Row structure

      iv. Creating and altering tables

      v. Row migration and chaining

      vi. Truncating rows vs deleting rows

      vii. Obtaining index information from the data dictionary

  b. Indexes

      i. Bitmap

      ii. B-Tree

      iii. Comparison of Bitmap vs B-Tree. Know which index to use based on application processing requirements.

      iv. Rebuilding vs coalescing

      v. Obtaining index information from the data dictionary

16. Database constraints

  a. Constraint states (validate, novalidate)

  b. Immediate and deferred constraints

  c. Primary and unique key enforcement

  d. Enabling and disabling constrains

  e. Constraint types

      i. Check

      ii. Primary key

      iii. Unique key

  iv. Not Null

17. Oracle account security

 a. Password management

 b. Account locking

 c. Account expiration and aging

 d. Password verification and history

18. Oracle profiles

 a. Security profile

 b. Performance profile

19. User management

 a. Default tablespace

 b. Temporary tablespace

 c. Tablespace quotas

 d. Data dictionary tables used to find user information

20. Security management

 a. System privileges

 b. Object privileges

 c. WITH GRANT vs. WITH ADMIN option

 d. Understand the difference between system and object privileges when a REVOKE statement is used.

 e. Know what privileges SYSOPER and SYSDBA have granted to them.

 f. Obtaining privilege information

21. Database roles

    a. Creating

    b. Granting

    c. Revoking

    d. Modifying

    e. Enabling and disabling roles

22. Database auditing

    a. Audit guidelines

    b. Auditing options

    c. Audit trails

23. SQL*Loader

    a. Direct load vs. conventional path load

    b. Control file specifications

    c. Data conversion

    d. Know the difference between a discarded record and a rejected record.

24. Globalization Support

    a. Database character sets vs. National character sets

    b. Guidelines for choosing a character set

If you have passed the two previous certification tests you are now an Oracle Certified Associate! To obtain an Oracle Certified Professional certification, you must pass the previous two tests and then take the Database Fundamentals II and Oracle Database Performance Tuning certification tests. Please note that you also have to take at least one instructor-led training test (see Chapter 1).

Oracle Certified Professional Tests

Exam 1Z0-032 – Oracle Database Fundamentals II

Oracle Database Fundamentals II begins with the basics of Oracle networking. The class (and the associated certification test) then covers Oracle backup and recovery (both RMAN and operating system) and ends with information on the Oracle Export and Import utilities. The certification test covers the following topics:

1. Oracle Networking

    a. Know the contents of the TNSNAMES.ORA, LISTENER.ORA and SQLNET.ORA files.

    b. Understand how the listener process works.

    c. Have a working understanding of the different Oracle Net connectivity options

        i. HTTP connectivity

        ii. Directory naming

        iii. Heterogeneous

        iv. Java client

    d. Know the basics (and differences of) Oracle Net Manager and the Oracle Net Configuration Assistant

    e. Oracle Connection Manager

    f. You must know how the Shared Server (previously called multi-threaded server) works and how it differs from a dedicated server process.

g. Shared Server architecture
   i. Parameters used to configure Shared Server
   ii. Dispatchers
   iii. Queue processing
   iv. Shared server processes
h. Know how to generate logs and traces on both the client and the server
i. Understand the basic LSNRCTL commands
j. Naming methods
   i. Host naming
   ii. Local naming

2. Backup and Recovery Overview
   a. Know the categories of failures and how they occur
      i. Statement level failures
      ii. User process failures
      iii. User errors
      iv. Instance failures
      v. Media failures
   b. Requirements to set up a successful backup and recovery strategy
      i. Business requirements
      ii. Operational requirements
      iii. Technical Requirements

Oracle Certified Professional Tests

3. Oracle recovery components. Know how the work together and how they are used for database consistency and database recovery.

   a. Redo log buffer

   b. Online redo logs

   c. Archived redo logs

   d. Checkpoint processing. Know what happens when a checkpoint is executed and the types of checkpoints (full, incremental, partial)

   e. Control files

   f. Data files

4. You must know the processing that occurs for the two phases of database recovery

   a. Roll forward phase

   b. Roll back phase

5. Tuning Oracle instance recovery

   a. Fast start on-demand rollback

   b. Initialization parameters influencing checkpoints

      i. *fast_start_mttr_target*

      ii. *log_checkpoint_timeout*

      iii. *log_checkpoint_interval*

   c. Understand how to use *v$instance_recovery* to estimate instance recovery times

6. Database archiving

a. You must have a strong understanding of the impact that archiving/noarchiving has on the types of recoveries that can be performed.

b. Starting the database in archivelog mode

c. Know what happens when the database is in archivelog mode but the ARCH process is not started.

d. Understand the following archive parameters:

   i. *log_archive_start*

   ii. *log_archive_dest_n* You must know the options used with this parameter

   (1) MANDATORY vs OPTIONAL

   (2) REOPEN

   iii. LOG_ARCHIVE_FORMAT Know the different options and naming methods.

   iv. Know the difference between *log_archive_dest_n* and *log_archive_duplex_dest*

   v. *log_archive_min_succeed_dest*

e. Know what data dictionary and V$ tables are used to obtain archive information.

f. Know what information is displayed when using the "ARCHIVE LOG LIST" command.

7. Recovery Manager (RMAN) Overview

   a. Features

   b. Basic components

   c. Allocating channels

   d. Media management

e. Connection types

f. Understand the difference between using and not using a recovery catalog.

g. Know the information that RMAN stores in the target database control file.

h. RMAN commands

   i. CONFIGURE

   ii. SHOW

   iii. LIST

   iv. REPORT

   v. REPORT NEED BACKUP

8. Backups using RMAN

   a. Know the difference between a backup set and backup piece

   b. Understand the commands used to create backup sets and image copies

      i. Whole database backups

      ii. Tablespace backups

      iii. Incremental backups

      iv. Differential incremental backups

   c. Know the difference between an image copy and a backup set

   d. Know which files (and what combinations) can be included in a backup set (data, control, archive logs)

   e. Know how to use RMAN to back up the server parameter (SPFILE) file.

9. RMAN Recoveries
   a. Complete recoveries
   b. Incomplete recoveries
      i. Time based incomplete recovery
      ii. Cancel based incomplete recovery
      iii. Sequence based incomplete recovery
   c. Restoring datafiles to a new location
   d. Database recovery
   e. Tablespace recovery
   f. Recovery using a backup controlfile
   g. Recovering from the loss of current online redo log files
10. RMAN Maintenance
    a. CROSSCHECK command
    b. Deleting backups and copies
    c. Changing availability status for RMAN backups and copies
    d. Retention policy
    e. Creating and maintaining an RMAN catalog
       i. Understand the steps required to create an RMAN catalog
    f. Catalog maintenance
       i. RESYNC CATALOG command
       ii. Resetting a database incarnation.
11. User Managed Backups

a. Data dictionary and V$ tables used to identify files needed for backup.

b. Have a thorough understanding of all of the database files that should be included in the database backup.

c. Closed database backups

d. Open database (hot) backups

e. Understand what happens when a tablespace is placed in backup mode using the ALTER TABLESPACE .... BEGIN BACKUP statement is issued.

f. Have a working knowledge of what happens to tablespaces that are in begin backup mode during an instance failure.

g. Know how to end an on-line backup that has failed.

h. Control file backup commands

   i. ALTER DATABASE BACKUP CONTROLFILE TO TRACE;

   ii. ALTER DATABASE BACKUP CONTROLFILE TO filename;

12. Recovery in ARCHIVELOG mode vs recovery in NOARCHIVELOG mode. Understand how Oracle uses archives to replay database changes.

13. User managed recoveries

    a. Complete recoveries

       i. Data file loss

       ii. Online redo log loss

(1) Loss of single member of a multi-member group

(2) Loss of all members of a multi-member group

iii. Controlfile loss

(1) Loss of a single member when the database has multiple members

(2) Loss of all controlfile members

b. Incomplete recoveries

i. Why incomplete recoveries need to be performed

(1) Time based incomplete recovery

(2) Cancel based incomplete recovery

(3) Sequence based incomplete recovery

14. Relocating files to new locations during user managed recoveries.

15. Oracle Export/Import. The tests always have a few questions on the Oracle Export and Import utilities. Know how the utilities work and the various options you can use with them.

Exam 1Z0-033 – Oracle Database Performance Tuning

Oracle Database Performance Tuning covers the information and practices used to tune Oracle database environments. It is probably the most challenging test of the four. There will be a lot of questions on the V$ performance tables and the toolsets used to monitor database performance. The test includes questions on the following topics:

1. Overview of database tuning

   a. Common performance problems

   b. Steps to tune a database environment (see the Oracle Performance Guide for this information).

2. Diagnostics and Tuning Tools

   a. Alert log

   b. Background and user trace files

   c. Oracle Enterprise Manager Have a general understanding of what OEM features can be used to generate tuning information including Oracle Expert.

   d. Statspack You must know Statspack thoroughly. The majority of questions will be on Statspack and the V$ tables.

   e. V$ tables. Have a strong understanding of the data contained in:

      i. v$session_event

      ii. v$session_wait

      iii. v$system_event

      iv. v$filestat

   f. UTLBSTAT/UTLESTAT. Know the differences between BSTAT/ESTAT and Statspack

   g. Oracle Explain - Have a basic understanding of how to use the Explain command and the output it generates.

      i. Table scans

      ii.   Index scans

  h. Oracle traces and TKPROF

3. Tuning Oracle I/O

  a. Data buffer cache tuning

  b. Table scans vs. index lookups

  c. Locally managed tablespaces vs. dictionary managed

  d. Know what causes DBWR to flush data to the database data files

4. Know the impact the frequency of log switches has on database performance.

5. Buffer Cache Tuning

  a. Buffer cache parameters

      i.   Understand the difference between *db_block_buffers* and *db_cache_size*.

      ii.   *sga_max_size*

      iii. Non-standard tablespace block sizes and buffer cache parameters

  b. Know the calculation to determine the buffer cache hit ratio

  c. Understand what the different Oracle buffer pools are used for

      i.   DEFAULT

      ii.   KEEP

      iii. RECYCLE

  d. Know how to activate the buffer cache advisory and the contents of the *v$db_cache_advice* view

Oracle Certified Professional Tests

e. Know what happens when you cache an Oracle table

6. Shared Pool Tuning

   a. Know the various shared pool latches

   b. Have a thorough understanding of cursor sharing

   c. Know the difference between a hard parse and a soft parse

   d. Know how to activate the shared pool advisory

   e. Understand what impact cached execution plans has on shared pool performance.

   f. Know how to pin large objects in the shared pool (and why you would want to do it)

   g. Know the calculations to determine the library cache and data dictionary cache hit ratios

   h. Understand the impact that Shared Server (formerly known as Multi-Threaded Server) has on shared pool performance

7. Have a strong understanding of dynamic instance resizing.

8. Tuning the Log Buffer

   a. Know what causes LGWR to flush the log buffer to the current online redo log files

   b. Know how to reduce redo operations by using NOLOG options for SQL*LOADER and direct load inserts.

9. Tuning the Oracle Shared Server

   a. V$ tables used to monitor Shared Server Performance

       i. *v$shared_server_monitor*
      ii. *v$dispatcher*
      iii. *v$dispatcher_rate*
      iv. *v$circuit*

  b. Have a basic understanding of the Shared Server Architecture

10. Tuning Sort Operations

  a. Understand the difference between the *sort_area_size* and *pga_aggregate_target* when allocating memory for sort operations.

  b. Know the relationship between *pga_aggregate_target* and *workarea_size_policy*

  c. Understand how to use the *v$pga_target_advice* view to tune memory sort areas

  d. Understand the differences between temporary and permanent tablespaces for sort performance

  e. Know how to configure a tablespace for efficient sorting

11. Tuning Oracle9i Undo segments

  a. Understand the difference between automatic undo and manual undo management

  b. Know how to create and alter an automatic undo management tablespace

  c. Know the parameters used to activate automatic undo management

      i. *undo_management*
      ii. *undo_tablespace*

      iii.   *undo_retention*

    d. You must know the contents of *v$undostat* and how it is used to size undo segment tablespaces

12. SQL Statement Tuning

    a. Have a basic understanding of Oracle SQL statement hints

    b. Optimizer plan stability and stored outlines (definitely a few questions on this topic)

    c. Enabling and disabling SQL trace

    d. Know the command line parameters for TKPROF (and what it does)

13. Statistics

    a. Understand the impact that statistics have on the Oracle cost based optimizer.

    b. Know the difference between the cost and rule based optimizers

    c. There are always questions on histograms

    d. Automatic statistics gathering

    e. Know the basics of exporting and importing object statistics

14. Tuning Oracle Data Blocks

    a. Know the difference between manual freespace management and manual freespace management using PCTFREE/PCTUSED

    b. Understand the effects row chaining and row migration have on database I/O performance (and the difference between the two)

15. Oracle Indexes

a. You must know the differences between B-Tree and Bitmap indexes. You must also know which one to use to increase performance in a particular situation.

b. Know when to reorganize an index and when to use REBUILD vs. COALESCE

c. Know how to determine if an index is being used

d. Understand reverse key indexes and what problem they solve

e. Have a thorough understanding of Index Organized Tables. There are always a few questions on this topic.

16. Have a working understanding of Materialized Views

a. DBM_MVIEW package

b. Query rewrite

17. Have a general understanding of the Oracle Resource Manager

Once you have passed the DBAI and DBAII tests (and taken one Oracle instructor-led class) you are now an Oracle Certified Professional

Conclusion

As stated previously, this chapter was not intended to give you all of the information you need to pass the Oracle certification tests. That information alone would require a book several times this size. I have taken these tests numerous times and I felt that the topics contained in this chapter always seemed to show up as test questions. Use this chapter as a general study guide to ensure that you do not miss any important topics.

Turn to the Oracle classroom guides and third-party certification books for more information. Good Luck!

Book Conclusion

I hoped that you enjoyed the information provided in this book. I very much appreciate you taking the time to read my first attempt at writing a document of this size. Rest assured that I have tried my best to clearly explain each and every topic contained in these writings. I admire prolific writers like Don Burleson, Michael Abbey and Richard Niemic because I often agonize over every word.

As you now know, I am a strong advocate of the Oracle documentation. Read the Oracle manuals and trust the information they provide. They contain virtually everything you need to know to successfully administer an Oracle database.

I am also an avid proponent of detailed documentation, standards, formalized processes and structured approaches to database administration activities. They are truly the keys to creating a successful Oracle database administration unit. The selection of support-related technologies is important but it is the effective implementation and administration of those technologies that is critical to organizational success.

The Oracle database is wonderfully complex. With each new release, Oracle raises the competitive bar by which all future database servers will be judged. This rapid pace of new releases and new features will ensure our jobs as DBAs remain both challenging and interesting. Oracle Version10i will once again change the way we use Oracle software to address the needs of today's business applications. If I have learned one thing in 15 years, it is that I have never stopped learning. It seems that with each new release, I oftentimes feel that I am back at square one. What more could a technician ask for?

Those who have taken my classes know that I take my job as an Oracle instructor extremely seriously. The classes are often described as an Oracle "boot camp" (although I prefer Foot camp). I try to impart 15 years of tips, tricks and techniques so that my students don't make the same mistakes I did. If you take a class at our Pittsburgh training center, you'll have me as your instructor. If you do have me as an instructor – be prepared because long days with few breaks are common. I enjoy teaching and I will guarantee you that I'll make every effort to jam as much information as I can into the time we have together.

Thanks again and I'll see you in class!

Index

A

audit_file_dest 282
audit_sys_operations 281
audit_trail 282

B

BSTAT 55, 59, 200, 201, 202, 222
buffer_pool_keep 82
buffer_pool_name 81

D

Data buffer cache 84, 164
db_block_buffers .. 76, 81
db_cache_size 76, 113
db_create_file_dest .. 111
db_keep_cache_size ... 82
db_nk_cache_size 113
db_recycle_cache_size 82
db_verify 182
db_writer_processes .. 86
dba_col_privs 272
dba_data_files 98
dba_role_privs 272
dba_roles 272
dba_sys_privs 272
dba_tab_privs 272
dba_tablespaces 98
dba_temp_file 98

dba_undo_extents 121
dba_users 242, 272
dbms_flashback 235
dbms_redefinition 137
dbms_shared_pool.keep
.... 190
dbms_stats 202, 206
DBWR . 67, 85, 123, 164, 165, 166
dbwr_io_slaves 86

E

ESTAT. 55, 59, 200, 201, 202, 222

F

failed_login_attempts 278
fast_smart_mttr_target
.... 125

I

initial 128
initrans 91

J

java_pool_size 83

L

large_pool_size 83

Index **313**

LGWR 67, 124, 164, 165, 166
local 103
Log buffer 84, 164
log_buffer 84
log_checkpoint_interval 125
log_checkpoint_timeout 125

M

max_sga_size 76
maxtrans 91

O

optimizer_dynamic_sampling 206
optimizer_index_caching 145
optimizer_index_cost_adj 145
optimizer_mode 144, 145, 185
ORA-27100 71
ORA-27102 71
ORA-27123 71
ORA-27125 71
ORA-7250 69
ORA-7251 69
ORA-7252 69
ORA-7279 69
ORA-7339 69
oracle_loader 135

oracle_priority 194
oracle_sid 170

P

parallel_automatic_tuning 83
password_grace_time 278
password_life_time ...278
password_lock_time .278
password_reuse_max 278
password_reuse_time 278
password_verify_function 278
-pfile 73
PFILE 73, 74, 78
pga_aggregate_target 82, 96
proxy_users 273

Q

queue_privs 273

R

remote_os_authent 276
role_role_privs 273
role_sys_privs 273
role_tab_privs 272
Rollback/Undo segments 164

S

session_privs 273

session_roles 273
sga_max_size 76
shared_pool_size 82
shmmax 70, 71
shmmin 70
shmmni 70
shmseg 70
sort_area_retained_size
.... 96
sort_area_size 82, 96
spfile 73, 77
SPFILE 73, 74, 78
statistics_level .. 204, 205

U

undo_management ... 121
undo_retention . 121, 235

undo_tablespace 121
use_stored_outlines .. 189

V

v$backup_device 178
v$datafile 98
v$log 124, 126
v$log_history 126
v$object_usage 158
v$recoverfile 168
v$rollstat 121
v$segment_statistics . 204
v$segstat 204
v$segstat_name 204
v$shared_pool_advice
.... 205
v$tempfile 98

Index **315**

About the Author

Christopher Foot has been involved in database management for over 16 years, serving as a database administrator, database architect, trainer, speaker, and writer. Currently, he is employed as Senior Database Architect and Senior Oracle Instructor at Contemporary Technologies, Inc. in Pittsburgh, PA.

Chris began his career working as a database administrator at Mellon Bank. For ten years at Mellon, Chris served as a DBA and later as the bank's Client Server Systems Architect. During his tenure at Mellon, Chris was responsible for helping to create Mellon's support infrastructure for all non-mainframe database applications. As a result, Mellon was asked by the Oracle Corporation to participate in Oracle's Showcase Environment program in August of 1996.

He broadened his skills at Alcoa, learning the world of manufacturing and became Alcoa's Database and Server Architect in April 1998. Chris was responsible for database and hardware server strategies at a corporate level, reporting to Alcoa's Chief Technology Officer (CTO) and Chief Information Officer (CIO).

Chris is the author of over twenty articles for a variety of magazines including DBAZine, Database Programming & Design, The Data Administration Newsletter, and Edge- The Database Survival Guide.

Chris developed Oracle and DB2 database training curriculum for several companies, including Platinum Technologies and KCS Inc. At Platinum, Chris was responsible for creating their entire Oracle curriculum including classes on general administration, backup/recovery, database tuning and several SQL and PL/SQL courses.

Chris is a frequent lecturer on the database circuit and has given over a dozen speeches to local, national and international Oracle User Groups. In addition, Chris has also been a guest lecturer for the Master's Program at Duquesne University. He was a featured speaker at six international Oracle User Groups, and four Oracle Open Worlds. At Oracle Open World, he spoke to a group of more than 700 and was asked to provide an encore presentation on database tuning.

His practical knowledge of databases has also made him a popular trainer. Chris received his Senior Oracle Instructor title in 1999, and was the recipient of Oracle's Oracle Approved Education Center Quality Achievement Award in 2000.

In his current position at Contemporary Technologies, Chris continues his training and writing while helping to manage databases for CTi's customers. CTi is one of only twelve Oracle Approved Education Centers in the country, allowing them to teach Oracle's own curriculum. CTi also provides remote database management services that help companies reduce costs and improve the health of their databases. Chris and the RemoteDBA team manage over 500 production databases for CTi clients. RemoteDBA has helped these companies maintain their focus on their core competency while outsourcing the day-to-day management of the databases. The result is higher database availability, better efficiency, at lower costs than traditional database support methods.

To read some of Chris's articles go to:
http://www.dbazine.com

Burleson Oracle Consulting

Oracle Training – This is a popular option for Oracle shops that want a world-class Oracle instructor at reasonable rates. Burleson-designed courses are consistently top-rated, and we provide on-site Oracle training and Oracle classes at standards that exceed those of other Oracle education providers.

On-site Oracle consulting – Don Burleson is available to travel to your site for short-term Oracle support. Common on-site Oracle consulting support activities include short-term Oracle tuning, Oracle database troubleshooting, Oracle9i migration, Oracle design reviews and Oracle requirements evaluation support. Oracle support and Oracle consulting services are priced by the hour, so you only pay for what you need. These one-time Oracle consulting services commonly include:

- Answering questions from your Oracle DBA technical staff
- Repairing down production Oracle database systems
- One-time Oracle tuning
- Installation of Oracle application packages

Oracle Tuning – Don Burleson wrote the book on Oracle tuning and specializes in improving Oracle performance on Oracle8, Oracle8i and Oracle9i. His best-selling Oracle performance books include *High-Performance Oracle8 Tuning*, *Oracle High-Performance tuning with STATSPACK*, and *Oracle High-Performance SQL Tuning* by Oracle Press. Don Burleson also specializes in Oracle SQL tuning.

Oracle Monitoring – As the author of the landmark book *Oracle High-Performance Tuning with STATSPACK*, Don Burleson offers a complete Oracle monitoring package, installed and tested on your server.

Oracle Project Management – Don Burleson provides complete Oracle design, starting from the initial concept all the way through implementation. Burleson has a proven history of designing robust and reliable Oracle database architectures and can recommend appropriate hardware, software, tools, and Oracle support.

Oracle Data Warehouse Design & Implementation – As the author of *High-Performance Oracle Data Warehousing*, Burleson is often called upon to provide Oracle DBA support for Oracle8 data warehouse projects.

Oracle Design and Oracle Performance Reviews – This is great insurance before your Oracle database goes live. The review ensures that your application will be able to support production user volumes and that it will perform according to your specifications. Burleson is also expert at Oracle scalability, and he can conduct stress testing to ensure that your production database will be able to support high-volume transaction rates.

Oracle New Features Planning – This is a popular service where your specific needs are diagnosed and specific Oracle8i and Oracle9i features are identified for your database. We also provide upgrade services for Oracle applications, including 11i.

Oracle Applications Support - We offer world-class Oracle Applications support and offer the best rates for upgrading Oracle Applications, including 11i.

Remote Oracle DBA Support - BEI Remote DBA offers world-class remote Oracle support for companies that are too small to have a full-time Oracle DBA.

Burleson Oracle Consulting also has a vast network of Oracle consulting contacts and we can supply Oracle professionals for all Oracle projects, from short Oracle engagements to large-scale Oracle projects. BEI only employs consultants with extensive experience and knowledge.

For Corporate Consulting & Training Call Toll Free 866-729-8145

www.dba-oracle.com

Burleson Oracle Consulting
Leader in Oracle Training & Consulting

Oracle9i RAC

Oracle Real Application Clusters Configuration and Internals

Mike Ault & Madhu Tumma
ISBN 0-9727513-0-0
Publication Date - June 2003
Retail Price $59.95 / £37.95

Combining the expertise of two world-renowned RAC experts, Oracle9i RAC is the first-of-its-find reference for RAC and TAF technology. Learn from the experts how to quickly optimizer your Oracle clustered server environment for optimal performance and flexibility.

Covering all areas of RAC continuous availability and transparent application failover, this book is indispensable for any Oracle DBA who is charged with configuring and implementing a RAC clusters database.

Mike Ault is one of the world's most famous Oracle authors with 14 books in print, and Madhu Tumma is a recognized RAC clustering consultant. Together, Ault and Tumma dive deep inside RAC and show you the secrets for quickly implementing and tuning Oracle9i RAC database systems.

http://www.rampant.cc/